SHADOW TO LIGHT

*Transformational Journeys
From Abuse & Betrayal
To Empowerment*

By Sasha Samy, MA

Copyright © 2013 by Sasha Samy
Second Edition – April 2013

ISBN
978-1-77067-383-0 (Hardcover)
978-1-77067-384-7 (Paperback)
978-1-77067-385-4 (eBook)

All rights reserved.

Disclaimer: The author of this book does not dispense medical advice or prescribe the use of any technique as a form of treatment for physical, emotional, or medical problems without the advise of a physician, either directly or in directly. The intent of the author is only to share information, tools and techniques she has used on herself, to help you in your quest for emotional and spiritual well-being. In the event, you use any of the information in this book for yourself, which is your constitutional right, the author and the publisher assume no responsibility for your actions.

No part of this publication may be reproduced in any form, or by any means, electronic or mechanical, including photocopying, recording, or any information browsing, storage, or retrieval system, without permission in writing from the publisher.

Published by:

FriesenPress
Suite 300 – 852 Fort Street
Victoria, BC, Canada V8W 1H8

www.friesenpress.com

Distributed to the trade by The Ingram Book Company

What is to Give Light must Endure Burning!
Victor Frankel

To God

I express my gratitude to You for giving me the courage and strength to bring this project to fruition. You have sustained and uplifted me when I have faltered, assured me when I was besieged with doubts. Without your love and grace, I would not be where I am today.

Amen!

To My Family and Friends

To both my children, whose love and support I appreciate immensely, I am proud of you for who you are. To my husband, thank you for listening, for your patience and encouragement. To my ex-husband, thank you for gifting me with two beautiful children. To all my loving siblings and wonderful friends who have supported me along my journey, I love you all! I give special thanks to screenwriter, Michael Bruce Adams and Dr. Matilda Gabrielpillai for their invaluable suggestions. I would also like to thank Dr. Gabrielpillai for proofreading my manuscript. For all the people who have made this book possible, I thank you.

Contents

TO GOD

AMEN!

TO MY FAMILY AND FRIENDS

INTRODUCTION. ix
DIVINE GUIDANCE: TRAJECTORY FOR THIS BOOK

PART I: PERSONAL STORIES

Chapter 1 3
STACY: UNDER THE FLAME OF THE FOREST TREE

Chapter 2 9
PARENT/DAUGHTER RELATIONSHIP:
THE BEGINNING OF A FRAGMENTED CHILDHOOD

Chapter 3 19
BONDING WITH BEST FRIEND AND SIBLINGS: PILLARS IN ADVERSITY

Chapter 4 23
MARRIAGE TO STEVEN: TRAVERSING THE FLAMING FOREST

Chapter 5 33
LIFE WITH STEVEN: THE DESTRUCTION OF SELFHOOD

Chapter 6 43
THE CALL OF THE UNIVERSE: DREAM ENCOUNTER WITH DARK ANGEL

Chapter 7 47
DISILLUSIONED: SUCKED INTO THE QUAGMIRE OF ABUSE

Chapter 8 51
FATE TAKES A TURN FOR THE WORSE: STANDING BY STEVEN

Chapter 9 55
MOVING FORWARD: EMBRACING THE FLAME OF HOPE

Chapter 10 59
MIRIAM: A KINDRED SOUL IN DISTRESS

Chapter 11 67
JASAREEN AND TESSA: ABUSE KNOWS NO BOUNDARIES

PART II: THE RUBRICS OF ABUSE AND BETRAYAL

Chapter 12 87
WHAT CONSTITUTES ABUSE?

Chapter 13 103
THE EFFECTS OF ABUSE: THE DISINTEGRATION OF SELFHOOD

PART III: THE JOURNEY TO HEALING AND SELFHOOD

Chapter 14 117
SELF-AWARENESS: THE KEY TO TRANSFORMATION

Chapter 15 123
SELF-KNOWLEDGE: THE PATH TO A CONSCIOUS LIFE

Chapter 16 135
JOURNEY INTO THE SOUL: UNMASKING AND
EMBRACING OUR SHADOW SELF

Chapter 17 145
SELF-REFLECTION: IDENTIFYING CORE EMOTIONS AND BELIEFS

Chapter 18 163
INNER WORK: THE INTEGRATION OF THE
CONSCIOUS AND UNCONSCIOUS MIND

Chapter 19 191
FORGIVENESS: THE POWER OF THE SACRED HEART

Chapter 20 201
LOVE: THE GREATEST ENERGY OF ALL

Chapter 21 205
UNITY CONSCIOUSNESS: LOVE THY NEIGHBOUR AS THYSELF

Epilogue. 211
MY SPIRITUAL JOURNEY: I AM WHO I AM

Bibliography. 215
About the Author. 219

INTRODUCTION

Divine Guidance: Trajectory For This Book

Shadow To Light is the manifestation of divine guidance I received in 2007 through a series of meditation. My personal experience of emotional abuse, as well as my encounters with other women of abuse, provided me with the impetus to heed the clarion call of the Universe to fulfill my soul's purpose. I come forward to share the stories of the four women mentioned in the book, so that others who are in a similar predicament will know that they are not alone, that they can exercise 'conscious choices' that can liberate them from their situation, and heal and reclaim their power and selfhood.

Personal transformation from within is the key to empowerment. It initiates a change in consciousness in the individual. 'Inner work,' as it is known, entails working on what Swiss psychologist, C. G. Jung, calls the "personal unconscious" or shadow self. Most of us go though challenges and trials in life that manifest in myriad forms: abusive or dysfunctional relationships, addictions, loss of loved ones, loss of employment, loss of property, accident or divorce. These challenges, which emerge as periods of darkness in our lives, often offer us opportunities for growth and re-birth.

In order for us to live from a lightened space of our authentic presence or true Self, we must allow our light or conscious aspect to shine on our shadow or unconscious aspect to be integrated into wholeness. It is therefore important for us to realize that we have the infinite potential within us to transform ourself and our environment, thereby reducing pain and suffering for ourself and for others. In doing so, we set into motion an evolutionary process that elevates us naturally to a higher expression of ourself. It is only personal transformation that will, ineluctably, lead to the raising of social and global consciousness. As such, it is our personal and social responsibility as individuals to heal and transform ourselves, to unblock and remove the barriers to our inner peace and happiness. It is only in making ourself available and open that we can move forward to appreciate the inherent goodness in life.

I use the motifs of 'shadow', 'light', and 'fire' throughout the book to reflect the essential transformational process of moving from the shadowland of dysfunctional relationship with oneself and with others to a lightened space of authentic power. By embracing the light of change and growth, we are choosing to dance with the sacredness of life that can pave the way for us to live with new hope, new life, new strength, new love and new possibilities.

My own healing and spiritual journey necessitated that I traverse the inner recesses of my psyche to confront and embrace my shadow self and allow my authentic self to emerge. Although my spiritual journey began when I was a young girl, it was in the year 2000 that I earnestly pursued an inner spiritual life. I spent much time soul-searching, reflecting, journaling, praying, meditating, reading books on psychology and spirituality, practicing energy healing, and walking and meditating in nature. In diligently turning inward, I learned gradually to open my heart to myself and to others: to accept that which I cannot change, to change what I can, and to forgive.

Abuse is not a topic that is openly mentioned, let alone discussed. It has been encapsulated by a 'patriarchal code of silence', which sadly promotes the very violence that it publicly ignores. The writing of this book is therefore an exercise in negotiating the 'silence' inherent in abuse and betrayal. Intimate relational abuse, prevalent in all countries, is one of those closed-door subjects that needs to be brought to the fore-front as it cuts across boundaries of nationality, ethnicity, age, gender, sexuality, education, social class and marital status (*WHO*, 2011). Studies show that one woman in every three around the world is abused either physically, sexually or psychologically by an intimate partner. In Canada alone, over 50% of Canadian women have reported experiencing at least one incident of physical or sexual violence (*WAVAW*, 2011). Although a greater percentage of the targeted in intimate abusive relationships are adult and teenage females, it is important to recognize that adult and teenage males and gay couples have also found themselves to be targets of abuse.

A common fallacy surrounding abuse is that it must be physical to be considered as one. Unfortunately, there are many teenage girls and women who do not even realize that they are in an abusive relationship because of the emotional or psychological nature of the abuse. Abuse often manifests itself in verbal, sexual, financial, spiritual and emotional or psychological behaviour. While bullying and infidelity are considered emotional abuse, self-destructive behaviours that manifest as addictions for instance, fall within the category of self-abuse. Abuse in any form is unacceptable. It is a violation of human rights. It corrupts the human spirit and robs both the perpetrator and the targeted off dignity and self-respect. The cycle of abuse however can only be broken if people are able to recognize the characteristics of abuse and not dismiss certain behaviours or attitudes as 'normal' due to cultural and social conditioning.

There is a dire need for more respect, education, social awareness and action to eliminate all forms of abuse. If each individual does his or her part in breaking the silence encoded in abuse, and in imbuing the basic value of 'respect' for one another, we will live in a better world where respect and reverence for the sacredness of life will become the norm.

The importance of shattering this silence cannot be overemphasized. It is silence that perpetuates the cycle of abuse and makes it difficult, especially for women of abuse to articulate their experiences, for fear of washing dirty linen in public and of public judgment. But as feminist writer Helene Cixous says, women must muster the courage break the "snare of silence," for it is silence that immobilizes us; it is silence that keeps us entrapped in our self-imposed prisons.

Testimony, on the other hand, can draw attention to abuse as a reality. Otherwise, abuse becomes something that society can easily deny as a social reality, which in turn poses a danger to targets of abuse and violence.

The first step to attaining empowerment comes with self-awareness, when one first recognizes and acknowledges that one is in an abusive or dysfunctional relationship. The next crucial stage is when one is able to exercise appropriate choices to change the status quo. Sharing one's experience is a powerful way of creating awareness and knowledge: it acts as a vehicle in raising the social and spiritual consciousness of men and women.

By taking the appropriate steps to heal, by making conscious choices to empower themselves and by seizing every opportunity to fulfil individual expression and creativity, be it in the private or public arena, women of abuse can move forward to redefine themselves, their experiences and reality and in the process, reclaim their selfhood.

Structure of the Book

Those who have experienced abuse, betrayal, addictions and other forms of dysfunctional relationships or who know persons who have experienced them or are interested in personal and spiritual development may find this book useful.

The book draws on personal anecdotes, research, psychology and spiritual teachings to offer a practical and holistic approach to recovering from abuse and aids in unblocking the barriers to living a more empowering and authentic life.. It is divided into 3 sections, with each part using a different approach. While Part I deals with personal narratives, Part II is research-based. It looks at the varied forms of abuse and their effects. Part III encompasses a holistic approach to healing and transformation. The best way to read the book is chronologically although Part II can be read on its own. You may find some overlapping of information in the three sections as examples in Part II and Part III are drawn from the personal anecdotes in Part I. You will also find that an upper case 'S' is used to distinguish the inner true Self or authentic Self from the outer or personality self.

Part I: Personal Stories

Part I delves into the fictionalized true experiences of four women: Stacy, Miriam, Jasareen and Tessa, with much of the focus on the first person narrator of the book, Stacy. It traces Stacy's life journey from her fragmented childhood experiences in the early1960s, through her unhappy and emotionally abusive marriage and its culmination in divorce. The action takes place in Singapore and moves to Canada. The four women who meet in Singapore are of different nationalities and come from all walks of life. The stories focus on their transformational journey of learning how to transcend their experiences of abuse and betrayal and to emerge as stronger and more wholesome individuals.

Instead of using individual case studies, I have chosen to fictionalize and weave the true experiences of the four women into a single story in an attempt to make it more personable and to reflect a supportive female community. It also serves to circumvent the issue of libel, which is enmeshed into the social mechanism of 'silence' that denies the targeted a voice to articulate her reality. The time frame, names, places and nationalities have been changed to protect the identities of the people involved in the stories. Of the four stories, one is a composite.

Except for this Introduction, the brief synopsis to each section and the epilogue, the rest of the book is rendered through the subjective voice of the main narrator, Stacy.

Part II: Rubrics of Abuse and Betrayal

Part II is research-based. It defines briefly what constitutes intimate relational abuse and betrayal. It looks at the reasons for why abuse takes place, the effects of abuse, the reasons why the targeted do not leave their partners and what is lacking in a dysfunctional relationship. Although society has yet to recognize emotional infidelity as adultery, there is a small section on it as it denotes abuse of trust and commitment. The purpose of this section is to create individual and social awareness of the characteristics of abuse, the conditions in which it thrives, and its impact on the individual and society at large. Violence, whether it occurs in the private or public sphere or global arena, is a violation of human rights that has universal repercussions. As discussed in the last chapter of this book, it is only in the healing and transformation of the individual that families, communities, societies, nations and the planet can be healed.

Part III: The Journey to Healing and Selfhood

Part III traces Stacy's personal journey to healing and selfhood. It emphasizes a holistic approach that includes psychology and spiritual teachings as means to focus on the crucial elements of healing, transformation and renewal. The holistic approach stresses the importance of integrating the mind, body and soul as part of a whole.

This section explores the concepts of rebirth and selfhood through the act of turning inward to look within one's self. Inner work is used to approach the 'shadow self,' which needs to be embraced with one's inner light or conscious self and integrated into wholeness. It is also used to re-examine the erroneous nature of belief systems within which one is currently operating in order to attain self-awareness and pave the way for self-acceptance, self-love, surrender and forgiveness. As such, this section attempts to show that journeying through these essential facets of healing and growth elevates the individual to an inner space of empowerment and authenticity.

Conclusion

The key to healing and selfhood is in the transcending of the experience of abuse and betrayal. I invite you to walk through this journey in redefining your reality by making conscious choices that will liberate you from your self-imposed prison, help you to break out of your self-destructive behaviour patterns and release you from the ravages of unforgiveness, resentment and bitterness that sucks both the perpetrator and the victim into the soul-destroying quagmire of hatred, suffering and revenge. I invite you to traverse the inner recesses of your heart and to ride on the wings of compassion and forgiveness for yourself and for others. I share with you these women's stories in the hope that in their healing and transformation, you will find yours!

Blessings!
Sasha Samy
Vancouver, BC.

PART I: PERSONAL STORIES

This section depicts the fictionalized account of the true experiences of Stacy, who is the main narrator of the book, Miriam, Jasreen and Tessa, whom she befriends in Singapore. It traces Stacy's life journey from her unhappy childhood and a tumultuous and emotionally abusive marriage to the dissolution of that marriage in divorce. The stories focus on how the four women transcend their abusive relationships and self-destructive behaviours to heal and restore their broken spirit.

The purpose of the narratives is to reflect not only the different layers of severity that abuse can manifest, but also the common trends and characteristics inherent in abusive relationships. It is in recognizing and educating oneself of the dynamics of such relationships that creates the awareness for one to initiate personal change.

Chapter 1

Every experience is a paradox in that it means to be absolute, yet is relative; in that it somehow always goes beyond itself and yet never escapes itself.

T.S.Eliot

Stacy: Under the Flame of the Forest Tree

Like everyone else, I too have a story to tell. I had been living in a limbo for the past forty-five years, going through the mechanics of what we call life. But now, as I stand on the beach at the break of dawn, listening to the gentle lapping of the waves, the chirping of the birds, feeling the chill of fresh dew on my skin, I make a solemn promise to myself to celebrate life. As I stand watching the beauty of nature unfold before me, voraciously savoring every moment, I gasp with joy as I take a deep breath of the crisp, salty air, feeling my whole body tingle with the life force of nature.

   Feeling alive and invigorated, I watch with abated breath, the sun peeping out from the horizon, splashing its azure, crimson fingers across the sky. What a sight to behold! A sight so splendid that I feel my heart expand with joy; a sight so endearing, so breathtaking that I can only gasp in awe and feel gratitude for being alive to experience nature's splendour. Words cannot express the infinite joy that one feels when one is in unity with all of creation!

As I stand there in total submission, with introspective reverence for God's creation, I think about my life, travelling back to the time when I was two years old. Looking at the journey of my life, I have come to realize that life is nothing more than a sum of one's experiences, positive or negative, as we choose them to be. When viewed from this perspective, life becomes a continuous journey of discovery and creation. Every moment is a choice to create what we want in our lives.

But how we choose to create each moment depends on our past history: the shared experiences, positive or negative, that we have had with our family, friends, teachers, colleagues and even strangers with whom we had come into contact on a daily basis; the attitudes and social and cultural beliefs that have been encoded in our subconscious mind, which we accept unquestioningly as our eternal truths; and the level of awareness and understanding we bring to these experiences.

I was two years old when my brother, Patrick, was born. Everyone doted on him, especially my mother, who had been longing for a son after having had four daughters. I remember standing at the doorway of my parent's bedroom, watching my family members crowding around him the day my parents brought him home from the hospital. I could not understand what the fuss was all about. Nobody seemed to notice me. I felt sad and lonely.

After a while, feeling ignored, I drifted out quietly into the garden and sat alone by myself on the grass, contentedly playing with the flaming red petals from the flowers of the tropical Flame of the Forest tree, which were strewn all over the grass like red velvet carpet. The splendour of the red flowers has never failed to captivate me since I was a little girl.

I love the Flame of the Forest tree and I love the month of April in the tropics when all the flowers burst into blossom, painting the landscape in a kaleidoscope of colours. The sight of the Flame of the Forest tree has a special place in my heart. It evokes nostalgic memories of my childhood, living in Singapore in a modest black and white

Tudor colonial bungalow with a sprawling garden that sloped down to a wooded area at the back of my house while the front garden faced the sea.

I recall sitting on the lawn, totally engrossed with playing with the strewn flowers, delightfully throwing them all over myself when one of my sisters, having found me missing from the house, came out to look for me in the garden, and took me in to see my little brother. I came to adore Patrick deeply. I had been told about him before he was born and had looked forward to having a playmate but I could not comprehend at that time why all the attention had been diverted from me to my little brother. I felt ignored most times by my mother and resented it.

As we grew older, my brother and I spent much time playing with our neighbours in our garden. We had lots of tropical fruit trees, shrubs and ferns that made hiding out simply superb. There were also Frangipani trees with white and pink flowers, pink Oleander shrubs and lots of orange and crimson Bougainvillea bushes. The kaleidoscope of colours gave the whole garden a vibrant air. For me, this was my paradise, being one with the many colourful parakeets, magpies, squirrels, and even bats that attacked our tropical fruit trees and devoured the mangoes and papayas. It was wonderful being amidst nature. I was at my happiest then.

My childhood was spent playing imaginative games with my siblings, friends, and cousins who would visit us during the school vacation. We would sometimes hide under a huge shrub in the backyard, and pretend to be fairies and trolls. At other times, we would play hide-and-seek and police-and-thief or go swimming at the beach. My mother or sister would pack our lunch boxes and we would happily scamper down to the beach, lay out our mats and hungrily devour sardine or egg sandwiches under a huge and shady Sea Almond tree.

Our vacations were spent swimming and basking in the sun, looking like sunburnt street urchins. We also went foraging for fruit in the wooded area near our home. We were one with nature, happy and content in our escapades. Often, we would encounter insects, garden snakes and spiders while playing hide-and-seek. The sight of these creatures and our loud shrieks would intermittently draw us frantically out of our hiding places.

These were wonderful memories spent with my friends and siblings but yet, at a deeper level, for some strange reason, I would sometimes feel this gnawing sense of being alone and a deep and inexplicable sadness and emptiness would descend upon me. I could not understand why I felt this way. Some days, I would sit on the swing in the garden all by myself, engrossed in daydreaming, feeling totally alone and isolated. It was much later in my adult life that I came to understand the reason for my perpetual sadness.

When I was about ten years old, my father divulged to me that my mother had been taken seriously ill upon my birth. She had been in no condition to nurse and care for me for a long period of time. It was my father, my two older sisters, an adopted sister and an aunt, who took turns to care for me. I was told that I cried incessantly, which often drove my sisters frantic as they did not know how to pacify me. They were themselves in their mid-teens so I presume it must have been a difficult time for them as well. I suppose, I must have felt the loss of my mother's love and touch as a new born child. Later in my adulthood, as I read books on psychology, I came to understand that when a stable caregiver is missing from a new born baby's environment, the baby experiences confusion and anxiety, and fears of abandonment abound. This fear of abandonment, unfortunately, was to impact all my relationships, including the relationship I had with myself.

As time went on and I went to school, I became more withdrawn and shy. I spent more time reading and completing my homework rather than playing outdoors. Often, I would hear the laughter and shrieks of my siblings and friends coming from the garden and would long to join them. However, as I was often set piles of homework by my older sister, who had taken on the task of tutoring me since I had started attending school, I had to remain behind to complete my homework before I could join them. By the time I had completed my tasks, they would be finished with their games.

And so, I spent more time indoors, either reading, dreaming, doodling, watching television with my siblings, or talking with my father when he returned home from work. I always looked forward to this time with my father. Just watching him walk through the door would be enough to make me happy. My heart would lift up in that moment as I felt my whole world light up. My father was my world. I simply adored him.

Chapter 2

There is only one happiness in life—to love and to be loved.

George Sand

**Parent/Daughter Relationship:
The Beginning of a Fragmented Childhood**

My father was a man of stature and dignity, much respected and loved by family, friends and colleagues. Although trained in accountancy, he worked as an administrator in the British Civil Service before Singapore became an independent state in 1965. A generous and warm-hearted man, my father often helped people in times of adversity, even to the extent of extending our home to friends who found themselves without a roof over their heads. We housed many families over the years.

In fact, both my parents were very hospitable and magnanimous people, who would never decline to help friends and relatives in need. My father had many friends from all walks of life. Even the office attendants and taxi-drivers that he befriended were invited home for meals. Since we often had unexpected guests dropping by our home for meals, my mother would always be prepared with extra food. I recall the huge pots in which she used to prepare her food, especially on festive seasons, when the house would be open from morning to night for friends and relatives to drop by for a meal.

My father was an understanding and broad-minded man who was willing to adapt and change with the times. Many of his nephews, nieces and friends' children who could not relate with their parents because of their rigid adherence to traditional Asian cultural beliefs, would seek his advice and look to him to be the mediator between them and their parents.

I enjoyed spending time with my father. It was for me, one of the most interesting and stimulating interactive moments I could possibly have. He was widely read, knowledgeable and an interesting person to talk to. We often discussed philosophical issues relating to life, death, God, and afterlife, topics that captivated me even at the age of 12. Those were some of my happiest moments as he would play the devil's advocate in an attempt to encourage me to form my own opinions.

My father encouraged my siblings and me to express ourselves, which was not a very common thing to do in Asian families, especially for females. But then, we were not the typical traditional Asian family either, where patriarchy was the norm. This was the era of the early 1960s, where not many of the families encouraged their children to speak up, least of all their daughters, who were expected to be submissive. They strictly believed and adhered to the adage that children were meant to be seen and not heard. In addition to that, adherence to filial piety meant complete obedience to one's parents.

Although my father's encouragement had made me feel secure enough to express myself with him, I was nevertheless too timid and shy to express myself outside the security of my home. Besides attempting to build up my confidence, my father, an avid reader from a young age himself, introduced me to the world of English literature. I was exposed to writers like Thomas Hardy and D. H. Lawrence when I was 13 years old. I was by this time putting away my Enid Blyton adventure books to devour books by Agatha Christie and Sherlock Holmes. Watching him read avidly instilled in me a love for reading. My father was not only an active sportsman who enjoyed interactive sports in his free time, he also enjoyed catching up with friends after work.

His social life however became a source of contention between my parents. It was unfortunate that my parents had different personalities and educational levels, which proved problematic in the long run as they shared few common interests except for their love of movies. Theirs was not a love marriage but one that had been arranged. In the early 1930s, matchmaking had been the norm. The matchmaker would be called upon to find an appropriate suitor for the bride and a meeting would be set up for both the bride and groom and their parents. If the parties involved agreed to the match, the marriage would take place without any courtship.

My father had been almost 30 years old when he got married, rather late and unusual for his time. He had become the sole breadwinner of his family of 10 members after his father had passed on and had been contributing to the household coffers since the age of 13. Despite the financial difficulties he had faced in his early life, my father was determined to make a success of himself. He worked hard, put himself through an English medium education and rose quickly from an assistant administrator to become an Higher Executive Officer in the Civil Service. His English education, not common in that era, and his successful administrative career placed him high in the hierarchy of a society noted for its elitist attitudes. Raised to speak only English at home, we were inevitably influenced to some extent by British cultural norms, which unfortunately gained the disapproval of my future in-laws.

I admired and respected my father for his strength, kindness, love and wisdom. An unconventional man who did not adhere to traditional and superstitious beliefs, he nevertheless ingrained in us the values of filial piety and respect for our elders. It seems to me now however that, though filial piety may be a virtue and a blessing in keeping familial relationships intact, it can, as I was to find out later in my interactions with my in-laws, be a curse when it limits your ability to voice your beliefs. It can be ensconced so deeply into your subconscious mind that it can influence you into behaving in a way that limits your choices and curtails your freedom of expression and your experience of selfhood.

It seemed natural that I should grow up feeling closer to my father than to my mother. I could relate to him better and was totally attached to him. My mother, by contrast, appeared to me distant, undemonstrative and mechanical. Sensing her lack of interest in me, I unconsciously drew away from her and clung to my father instead. This made things worse for me as I felt that she somehow resented the fact that I favoured my father over her. My mother and I never got along well until I married and left home.

There were times as a little girl when she would pick on me for things that went wrong in the home even if it was not my fault. Sometimes, my younger brother or sister would break or spill something but they would be let off while I took the blame for it. No matter how much I protested, I would be scolded or punished. I felt angry at her unfairness and resented her even more.

My mother was also prone to erratic mood swings. At that time, I could not fathom why she would oscillate from being gentle one moment to becoming bad-tempered the next. At other times, she would become withdrawn and depressed. She was unpredictable. It was hard to gauge her moods no matter how closely I watched her. To me, she seemed different from other mothers, distant and unreachable. Her silence, like a formidable fortress erected around her, stood as a barrier between her and me. I just wanted my mother to be like other mothers: I wanted her to love me, to touch me, to cuddle me. I wanted to reach out to her, to draw her into my world, to have her look into my eyes and notice me. I wanted to see her laugh, be happy and joyful.

I did not want this silent, sad and angry mother. Neither did I want to see those deep pools of sorrow or bursting rage in her eyes. Everytime I witnessed the anguish in her eyes, I wanted to run away and hide from them. I could not bear to feel her unhappiness, her pain, her sorrow that struck a chord deep in me. The rare times when I found her cheerful and happy were when our family friends visited us: the adults would play cards while the children went outdoors into the garden to play.

I was told that almost one year after my birth, my mother recovered from her depression and was quite well in spite of her unpredictable mood swings until the year I turned 13. A severe hormonal imbalance precipitated her illness as she slipped into another debilitating depression. Things became tumultuous at home as I watched my mother retreat into a world of her own, slipping once again into a catacomb of pervasive silence. It was strange to see her tend to her chores, trapped in her tower of silence, sometimes staring at us vacantly, at other times, responding with lucid answers to our queries.

My siblings and I did not know how to respond to her. We were too young to understand what was going on with her: her erratic mood swings and unpredictable behaviour left us floundering in fear and misery. Her remoteness however kindled in me a burning desire to make contact with her, to penetrate through those walls and barriers she had constructed around her, to see what was going on in her mind. But it seemed like an impossible task to get close to her: she was unreachable.

I was angry with her for not being present, for not being the mother I wanted her to be. Then one day, my father took me aside and told me to be patient with her. He explained to me that she had suffered a difficult life as a child, orphaned at the age of five. Although she had come from a wealthy family, which had owned acres of real estate, she and her younger siblings had suffered much hardship and abuse from her guardian after the death of her parents. The guardian had squandered most of their wealth and had left her and her younger siblings with very little.

The sufferings, trauma and abuse she had suffered as a child from losing her parents and at the hands of her cruel guardian at a young age, then later, with a difficult mother-in-law in her teenage years, followed by an unhappy and incompatible marriage with my father, inevitably took an enormous toll on her mental and physical health. Unhappiness engulfed her. She suffered in silence for much of the time, as was expected of the women from her generation who did not have the level of education nor the financial independence and resources to exercise better choices for themselves. Instead, she battled on stoically under waves of overwhelming despair, anguish and isolation.

My siblings and I were deeply traumatized by my mother's depression, especially the younger ones. By this time, my older siblings had married and had left home. My father, who was seriously ill with heart problems, had gone for a couple of months to recuperate at his sister's home in neighbouring Malaysia, so I was left to look after my younger siblings. My youngest sister, Shannon, was only six years old then and my younger brother, Edwin, nearly eight. I felt a heavy load descend upon me as I assumed my mother's role as caregiver. My brother Patrick, who was only 11 years old then, provided me the much-needed support to help me cope with my two younger siblings.

Life became a journey of traversing a period of darkness. Unable to comprehend my mother's condition and the extent of her illness, we would watch her sit by the window and gaze for hours into space with unfocused and tortured eyes; she reminded me of a tortured animal, grappling and writhing with unspeakable pain. I would often surreptitiously observe her and wonder what was going through her tormented mind.

Often in this state of distraction, my mother would become oblivious of us. Then in a jolt, she would snap out of her dazed state and resume her chores. It was strange to see her behave in this way, zooming in and out of conscious reality. My younger siblings were afraid of her erratic mood swings and looked towards me for comfort. These were very painful times for us, watching our mother suffer deep torments of the mind and soul.

A sense of insufferable gloom pervaded my soul. I felt lost and incapable as a 13-year-old to do anything for her. Despite my anger at her for not loving me in the way I wanted and for not being the mother I wanted her to be, I loved her deeply and was greatly distressed that I could do nothing to relieve her of her angst except to take her for her medical appointments and care for my younger siblings.

As my mother's moods became more erratic, we lived with a constant gripping fear and tension of when she would fly into a rage. In those terrifying moments when she did, my siblings and I would hastily seek refuge in our bedroom. Often with hearts pounding, not daring to make a sound lest we attracted her attention, we would wait out the time, patiently reading or studying.

When hunger struck, Patrick would volunteer to race downstairs to the kitchen to grab some cookies for us to stave off our hunger since my mother would normally forget to prepare our meals in those moments. That was when I learned to prepare simple meals for us. Sometimes, which we preferred, Patrick would get take-out. Despite our intense fear that my mother might hurt us, she never once did.

I felt responsible for my younger siblings and tried my best to care for them. I was thankful that Patrick was always there beside me to give me the support I needed. The intensity of the tension and trauma of living with a mentally ill mother took its toll on us emotionally and physically. We had to cope with school, with the situation at home and with the stigma. It was not easy for us. Often consumed by an unreedemed dreariness, feeling distraught and overwhelmed, we jumped and panicked at every sound we heard.

We were literally living on the edge of darkness, becoming nervous wrecks in the process. I became paranoid about having my back to my mother lest she should strike me. My brother Patrick was so traumatized with the home situation that he had taken to stammering while my youngest brother, Edwin, was frequently falling ill with asthma. I too, found myself struggling with perpetual colds and fatigue. We were exhausted and desperate and felt lost and alone in our predicament. We did not know what to do or who to turn to for help.

One day, in my utter despair, I cried out in anguish to God to ask him why he was doing this to us: why was he making my mother and all of us suffer so much, why could we not be a normal, happy family. I could not bear to see my mother in this state and suffered deep agony when she suffered. Yet I continued to blame her unfairly for emotionally abandoning us again.

It never occurred to me then that my father too had, in a way, abandoned us at a crucial time when we needed him most. I was only too happy to blame my mother for our unrelenting suffering. It was much later in my life that I came to see and understand that it was no fault of hers, and how difficult it must have been for her. She was a sick and lonely soul, who was lashing out at the world in agony for the abuse and trauma she had suffered.

The difficult, painful and traumatic teenage years however left me reticent and painfully shy. I was growing up into this skinny, socially-awkward and self-conscious teenager. I felt unattractive and was too shy to extend myself socially. So, I sought the solace of my books instead. It felt much safer to stay in my cocoon than to venture out from it into new areas. I was even too self-conscious to participate in sports at school until I attended college and took up tennis, which boosted my self-confidence. Beset with constant fears of failure and ridicule, I felt imprisoned by my own irrational fears, which were not allowing me to grow as I should.

My soul was dying to get out into the world and to experience life and fun like any other teenager but I was too terrified to leave my comfort zone. I envied those out there living their lives. I had become a mere bystander, watching the world pass me by, overwhelmed by my home situation. I felt engulfed by the unhappiness at home, by my mother's depression, which I had felt was insurmountable and the heavy responsibility of looking after my siblings. Deprived of a normal childhood, I had to grow up quickly to assume responsibility for my siblings.

The lack of emotional bonding with my mother left me with a gnawing sense of emptiness, a void that was to continue into my adulthood. Starved of love, affection and nurturance, I longed deeply for a happy family. I longed for my mother's love and touch. I longed for laughter in my life. I wanted us all to be happy.

But there was no laughter, no fun, no joy, only pain, and more pain at seeing my mother ill and incapable of helping herself. Pain at seeing her deeply unhappy with my father and yet being unable to voice out her needs except through escalating quarrels that made her explode in rage from pent up emotion and frustration. And finally, pain at seeing the whole family suffer the consequences of her illness and an unhappy home.

Chapter 3

A friend is one that knows you as you are, understands where you have been, accepts what you have become, and still, gently allows you to grow.

Albert Schweitzer

Bonding With Best Friend and Siblings: Pillars in Adversity

Growing up in adversity in a conflict-ridden home with a mother who was prone to depression developed in me the same kind of stoic determination that I had observed in my parents. Difficult as things may have been in my home, I never once ran away from my responsibilities. Neither did I find solace by turning to substances, like alcohol or drugs to help me tide through my pain. I wonder if it was this inherent stoicism, the indomitable spirit in me that had kept me hanging on to my unhappy marriage later on. Whatever it was, I know that it was God's grace that kept me going, that gave me the strength to handle the challenges that were thrown in my path.

Fortunately, at this time, I had a best friend, Caitlin, who provided me with the emotional support and listening ear that I needed. I did not have many friends, just a few close ones. Socializing was not something that came naturally to me. Wary of getting too close to anyone, I often kept my distance, preferring to observe in silence instead. It was as if I feared being hurt and abandoned. When Caitlin and I met for the first time at our secondary school orientation, we immediately warmed up to each other.

Caitlin was bubbly, funny and outgoing. I was the quieter of the two, but with her, I felt alive. She was fun to be around. We lived in the same neighbourhood and enjoyed going for long walks, and visiting with each other in our homes. I shared most of my secrets, dreams and problems with her and she with me. Some weekends, we would catch the occasional movie or meal together. We were very close and I trusted her. She looked out for me at school. And I did the same for her.

By the time I was to attend college, my father had retired. I was 16 then and wanted to go to college, no matter what it entailed. Not wanting to burden my father, who had my three younger siblings to support, I borrowed money from my older sister and put myself through college. I was not going to give up on my dreams and was determined to face any obstacle in my path.

Both Catlin and I applied for the same college and were delighted when we were accepted. We spent the next two years as classmates and became even closer, often going on group dates. Eventually, we lost contact with each other when she left to study overseas. I will always treasure my friendship with Caitlin and hold fond memories of her in my heart. She was the one person who could make me laugh and be silly during those difficult years; her friendship made things bearable for me. The gap she left in my life would later be filled with another best friend, Rina, whom I met when we attended nursing college.

My Siblings and I in Early Adulthood

As my younger siblings and I grew up into young adults, we continued to uphold our family motto: united we stand, divided we fall. We supported one another in looking after our mother as she went in and out of hospital. My older siblings contributed financially but were not always physically present to care for her. By this time, my second sister was travelling overseas frequently on work assignments and my oldest sister had migrated. My third sister had her own family-related challenges to deal with but she nevertheless tried her best to help.

The four youngest in the family were left then to physically and emotionally care for our mother and aging father. It was reassuring for us to have my youngest brother, Edwin, live with my parents and to be close at hand to help them. While Edwin would take my father for his monthly medical appointments, with Shannon helping to shoulder his load, I would take my mother for hers. Each time my parents were hospitalized, we stood in unison and gave one another support.

But when it came to my mother's turn, it was never an easy task for us to have her committed to an institution. No matter how many times we went through the process, it was not something we could ever get used to. It was painfully unbearable for us to see our mother cry and plead with us not to leave her in institutional care. We suffered tremendously, besieged with overwhelming guilt and anguish. It felt as if we were betraying and abandoning her. It broke our hearts to see her in such great distress that we would end up hugging one another, sobbing our hearts out.

Fortunately, we had spouses who not only empathised with us but also stood by us and supported us in our journey with our mother until she died of cancer at the age of 68. Although relieved at the cessation of her suffering when she passed on, I grieved deeply, feeling greatly the loss of her presence in my life. My perspective of her had gradually changed as I came to accept her for who she was. I was able to appreciate her love not only for me but also for my siblings, for our children and spouses; every one of us had, in one way or another, been miraculously touched by her presence and love.

As a child, I had grown up believing that my mother had not loved me but it was my ex-husband, Steven, who had made me realize that she had but that I was unable to perceive it. It was only after I had gotten married that my mother's love for us became more apparent to me: she had kept in touch with us almost on a daily basis, had taught our live-in domestic helpers how to prepare our meals, ensured that our young children were well taken care of while we were away at work, and prepared sumptuous meals for us whenever we gathered at her home with our spouses and children.

My mother had become more peaceful, gentle and loving as she grew older. The angry person at war with herself and with the world at large had become almost non-existent by the time she passed away. She had, in fact, become more demonstrative with her affection, especially with her grandchildren. Her love for my children and my ex-husband, Steven, made up for the lack of bonding with me in the early years.

Both of my parents had treated Steven well and he, in return, not only respected them but was also affectionate with them. He had a particularly soft spot for my mother and I appreciated that. This was a part of Steven that I had loved most. He could be lovable, funny, kind, warm and generous to those in need but totally arrogant, brutally frank and harsh to those who disagreed with or displeased him. It was as if he had two sides to him like Jekyll and Hyde. Unfortunately, I was to see more of his Jekyll side in our marriage.

Chapter 4

I am what I am today because of the choices I made yesterday. The choices I make today will affect what I am tomorrow.

Anonymous

Marriage to Steven: Traversing the Flaming Forest

I met Steven when I was 18 and still at college. I married him four years later. We started off group dating with Caitlin and her boyfriend before embarking on single dates. I found Steven sporty, charming and intelligent. He had a great sense of humour and made me laugh. We would spend weekends at the beach with our group of friends or we would go for simple meals or to the movies. Even though we had a great time and were at the height of a passionate relationship, we were often quarrelling. Ours was what you would call a roller coaster relationship. It was emotionally charged, volatile and disruptive.

The problem was that we had different personalities. Steven was an extrovert while I was more of an introvert. He was inclined to the sciences and I, to the arts. He was athletic and enjoyed sports, spending time outdoors and socializing while I preferred reading, watching movies and attending stage plays, although I did develop an interest in tennis and golf later. Steven was confident and sure of himself while I was shy, sensitive and self-conscious. Our different perspectives of life inevitably sparked off quarrels between us.

I found Steven overbearing and arrogant and tried very hard to resist being dominated by him. All too soon, our relationship became a battleground for power. I held on to my beliefs and opinions and was not willing to change them just to appease him. He, on the other hand, could not accept that I had a mind of my own. The differences in our personalities and perspectives were to set the tone for the failure of our marriage. In hindsight, it appears to have been doomed right from the start.

To add to this, Steven's parents opposed our relationship. My future in-laws who were from mainland China disapproved of me because of my mixed heritage: Chinese and Portuguese descent. My family spoke mostly English with a spattering of Chinese and Portuguese while his family spoke mainly Cantonese. Being traditional, they displayed a strong affinity to their culture and disapproved of my English-speaking, westernized upbringing. They took an instant dislike to me and treated me with disdain. On my part, their traditional cultural beliefs, which were very different from my upbringing, made it difficult for me to integrate with the family. I felt cloistered and stifled with them. While I tried my best to be as cordial as possible, Steven's parents would either ignore me when I visited them or would be downright rude to me, often passing uncalled for remarks about me. I tried to ignore their indifference and abusive remarks for Steven's sake.

Initially, I spoke to Steven about this while we were dating in the hope that he would speak to his parents because I felt uncomfortable doing so. To engage in a war of words with them was just not in my nature. Although Steven appeared aggrieved to see his parents treat me unkindly, he did nothing to defend me from his parents' abuse.

What was I thinking? How could I not have heard the warning bells go off and realize that if he could not stand by me emotionally while we were dating, he would obviously not be there for me in marriage? I should have known that his lack of emotional support would continue even during our marriage.

True enough, Steven told me a couple of years later, "Go fight your own battles. Stop expecting me to fight them for you." It was not like he ever did anyway. As I recall, there were many evident signs for a bad marriage right from the beginning of the relationship but I had foolishly chosen to ignore them. My father had in fact cautioned me about the difficulty I might find in fitting in with his family because of their traditional ways but I took no heed of his advice. I was in love and wanted to marry Steven. I did not realize at that point of time that I was compromising my selfhood in marrying him.

Steven and I went ahead and got married in a simple wedding despite his family's objection. His mother made no attempt to hide her displeasure. Possessive of her son, my mother-in-law cried and made a fuss on our wedding day, typically I thought, in keeping with the histrionics of their tradition. She did the same thing when my first son was born. She visited me in hospital bearing an unhappy and sulky face, which made me wonder to myself if she was attending my funeral.

Steven's father, who became more amicable towards me after the wedding, was openly hostile towards me before that. He disliked having me anywhere near him. Once, I had unsuspectingly sat at the dining table with him to have my dinner and was caught totally by surprise to see the look of distaste on his face. He picked up his dinner plate immediately, glared at me angrily and walked away abruptly, leaving me feeling totally aghast.

It was unbelievable! I was treated like a pariah. I felt insulted, hurt and shocked by his behaviour. It was demeaning. I did not know how to react. So I kept silent, which was a huge mistake. I had at that time, no knowledge as I have now that their treatment of me was abusive. I knew it was wrong but abuse was not something that was mentioned or talked about openly. To me, it seemed inconceivable that people could treat others in this manner, especially since I came from a family where kindness and generosity knew no bounds.

I never told my father that he was right about my parents-in-law until one day, during one of my visits home, he told me that he had heard from a mutual friend that my in-laws were not treating me well. He wanted to know if it was true. I looked at him with tears in my eyes, too ashamed to say anything. I had naively believed Steven when he had assured me that his parents were wonderful and kind people, even before I had met them. So I had told my father that I was sure he was wrong about them when he had tried to caution me. I was young, naïve and in love, and too blind to see what I was getting myself into.

In the early years of our marriage, Steven and I made it a point to visit our respective parents almost every weekend. Although I did not look forward to our visits to his parents' home, I nevertheless accompanied him to make him happy and to accord them the respect that was expected of me as their daughter-in-law. Besides, all hell would have broken loose if I had refused to go along. Whenever I tried resisting, Steven would turn verbally abusive. Once, he even manhandled me, pulling me by my hair and forcing me out of the door. Other times, he would make me feel so guilty that I would be compelled to give in to him.

On these occasions, his mother would either pass caustic remarks that would upset me greatly or she would treat me like I was nonexistent. Steven of course did nothing to stop her. In spite of her poor treatment of me, Steven insisted that we visit them regularly so that our children could have a relationship with their grandparents. I was often apprehensive, tense and resentful during these visits. Their obvious disrespect of my personhood violated my sense of self; it left me feeling totally bereft.

Our marriage was, by this time, becoming increasingly strained. We were often quarrelling and I was unhappy. I was angry with him for his lack of emotional support in handling his parents' treatment of me. Silent rage and fury welled up in me, creating a chasm between us that was to widen beyond repair. This state of affair continued for almost eight years until I decided that I had had enough of it. I obstinately refused to keep up with the weekly façade of visiting them and kept my distance. Despite my anger at them, I encouraged Steven to visit his parents on his own as I felt he had a right to maintain a relationship with them, but somehow, he did not relish the idea.

After that, my contact with Steven's family was kept to the minimum. Even on those occasions when I did meet his mother, she took pleasure in taunting me with her snide remarks. Whenever they visited us at our home, I tried my best to be as cordial and as welcoming as I could possibly be. But I stood my ground and refused to let her interfere in the way I ran my home or raised my children. I politely ignored her caustic remarks and suggestions unless I felt they were reasonable or helpful.

My relationship with Steven's mother continued to be strained and painful until my second child was born, and then things miraculously changed between us. She would come over to my house to assist me with Emily, upon Steven's insistence because I had sustained complications during childbirth. Initially, although we were polite with one another, we tried to keep out of each other's way. Then one day, while we were chatting casually about my children, she decided to share some aspects of her life story with me. I was surprised to find her confiding in me.

Like my mother, she too had been orphaned young, in her teenage years and had gone through a difficult life. Her marriage to Steven's father had not been easy. He had been a difficult man who had neglected her emotionally in the early years of their marriage although he had been supportive of her in the later years of her life. He had spent hours away from the home and had left her alone to cope with her three young children. She had been lonely and miserable but had been fortunate to have the support of good friends.

As I listened to her, I felt deep empathy for this woman who had suffered much. Soon after this incident, she suffered a stroke and was never the same fiery woman that she had been before her illness. My anger at her for treating me badly and not accepting me for myself, dissipated. I could not go on resenting her. In fact, I felt sorry for her. Very often, those who react harshly are themselves in pain and feel unloved. Like my mother, my mother in-law had deserved better than what life had relegated to her.

In the meantime, my marriage was deteriorating rapidly. The first 10 years of my marriage had not been easy: there had been verbal, mental and some physical abuse from Steven. As I recall now, the abuse had started even before we had gotten married. Steven was charming and gentlemanly for the most part in the early years, but he had a fiery temper and, when he was riled up, he could turn quite nasty.

The first time he slapped me was before our marriage. We had quarrelled over his mother and I had complained about his not standing by me whenever she attacked me with insults. In my frustration and resentment, I angrily told him: "You are such a mama's boy. Maybe you should just remain with your mother since you are still attached to her apron strings." I heard Steven draw in his breath and felt a twitch of fear in my heart as I saw the fury in his eyes. I knew I had crossed a boundary and immediately regretted what I had said.

The next moment, before I knew it, I had received a resounding slap across my cheek. I was stunned. For a moment I glared at him, speechless. I was afraid, yet furious. Then I shouted at him, "Don't you ever do that again." At first, he glared at me defiantly, and then shouted back, "You have no right to say anything about me or my mother." Then he quickly softened and apologized. Little did I realize that once a man hits a woman before marriage, he is most likely to continue after marriage.

Soon after this incident, I returned my engagement ring to him after yet another nasty quarrel and told him not to return. But he did. He came back and returned the ring and I accepted it. I loved Steven and wanted to marry him even though I had misgivings about our relationship. I had felt something vital missing from the relationship; it was a longing for emotional connection that could not be assuaged. The lack of emotional bonding with the people I loved left me with a desire deep within me that beckoned my soul; a desire that I later came to understand as a longing for connection with my true inner Self. I clung on to the relationship, unable to break free from him, hoping instead for it to deepen over time. I had fathomed that what little emotional connection we had was better than no connection at all.

One month after our wedding, I knew the honeymoon was over. I was rudely jolted out of my fantasy world when Steven resorted to name-calling and hostile jokes during our quarrels. This was when I began to see more of Steven's Jekyll side. When I had first met Steven, I had been skinny and petite and he had complained that I had not enough 'meat' on me. He wanted me to put on some weight. And when I did gain some weight, Steven began to make subtle jokes about it. This soon gave way to more hostile jokes and name-calling.

In one incident, after an exchange of words, Steven who had gotten so angry with me, looked at me with disgust flashing in his eyes and shouted vindictively at me: "Just look at you! Look at your stomach: you look like a pregnant duck, and you waddle like one too! And that cellulite on your legs, it looks disgusting." Taken aback, I stood there for a moment, shocked and stunned by his cruel words. It felt as if he had plunged daggers deep into my heart.

There was an impregnable silence as I stared at him with unseeing eyes. I could feel the prickling of tears gathering in my eyes. I saw again, the look of utter disgust in his eyes. I closed my eyes to shut it out and felt a deep, wrenching pain pierce my heart. I choked back my tears and fled from the sitting room, where we had been having our afternoon tea. I locked myself up in my bathroom and sobbed my heart out. I could not forget the look in his eyes. I felt fat and ugly.

Since that time, Steven knew that the fastest way he could get back at me was through name-calling. He used it as a weapon whenever we quarrelled, knowing that I would be dumbstruck with pain and be unable to respond to his abuse. But I soon learned how to hit him below the belt, just as he did, to defend myself. Our relationship became more volatile and destructive over time. It became ugly.

Steven's name-calling and negative perception of me impacted me adversely. My greatest mistake was that I had put Steven on a pedestal. I had admired his intelligence, wit and humour and had been swayed by his smooth talk and charisma. Believing that he was the smarter of the two of us, I took every adverse remark he made of me seriously and began to believe over time that I was not 'good enough' or 'smart enough'. He often called me 'stupid' and 'useless', words that would constantly reverberate in my mind and, sad to say, over time, my self-confidence plummeted drastically.

Steven was often disdainful of my successes. Once, when I had jubilantly informed him that the poems I had written had been selected for publication in an anthology, he scoffed and replied, "Any fool can write a poem, so what's the big deal?" I was devastated. Something broke inside of me. The condescending remark hurt me so tremendously that I could not go on with my writing. Something in me shut down. I felt stupid, incompetent and discounted. When I think about it now, I wonder in amazement at how I could have given my power away to him, how I could have allowed his remark to affect me to that extent, but unfortunately, it did. It seared my heart.

Steven's verbal abuse continued over the years. In yet another incident, he laughingly called me a baby elephant and said that I was fortunate that he had not told his colleagues that he had a baby elephant living at home with him. I was mortified. He would often pass callous and condescending remarks that made me feel useless, hopeless and ugly. Often in a quarrel in the later years, he would shout at me, "You are a nothing! Remember that! You may have a Master's degree but it amounts to nothing because you have nothing to show for it." He would stress on every syllable of the word 'nothing' to emphasize his point.

Over the years, Steven's favourite target words to me were 'stupid', 'lazy' and 'hopeless'. In Steven's eyes, success was measured by one's occupation, remuneration and status, and it was obvious that I did not fit in with his idea of success as mine was a vocation: nursing. I may not have earned as much as those in the corporate world, like he did, nor was mine considered a glamorous job but, in my heart, I knew I was doing something meaningful with my life. Not only had I been excellent at what I was doing, I had also contributed and made a difference in my patients' lives, and that was sufficient for me.

The marriage worsened when I gave up my full-time nursing job for part-time work after my second child, Emily, was born. I had meant to devote more time to my children and also offer Steven, who was climbing up the corporate ladder, greater support. But what little respect he had for me disappeared with that: like many chauvinistic men, Steven did not recognize my contribution to the home nor my part-time nursing job as 'work.'

By this time, I was beginning to believe more and more of the things Steven said about me, although outwardly, I kept fighting it and proving to myself and to others that I was not stupid, that I was in fact, perfectly capable and competent. I kept pushing myself tirelessly to be the 'perfect' mother, wife, daughter, sister and nurse. Striving constantly to be better, I remained unhappy with my efforts. I was doing well in my post-graduate studies and excelled at my work. And yet, day by day, I was slowly breaking down inside. Steven's personal attacks on my selfhood were devastating me. He was breaking my heart and crushing my spirit.

Chapter 5

Things fall apart, the centre cannot hold;
Mere anarchy is loosed upon the world.

William B. Yeats

Life with Steven: The Destruction of Selfhood

Steven, a typical alpha male, was a hard, demanding and domineering man who could be callous, insensitive and self-absorbed as much as he could be dynamic, charming and charismatic. A super-achiever who is competitive by nature, Steven excelled in his endeavours and expected the same from his family. This placed an enormous strain on us as it caused us great anxiety whenever we felt we were not fulfilling his expectations. He was often highly critical of everything we did and said.

Steven's attempts to teach me how to swim, golf and rollerblade, more often than not, would end up in conflict. He always expected me to do things either faster or better and no matter how much I endeavoured, my attempts were never good enough for him. I felt pressured and tense most of the time and this made me feel angry and resentful. In retaliation, I became defiant and resistant, which inevitably sparked off more quarrels between us.

Steven was not only hard on me, he was the same with my older son, John, who had my temperament. When John was five, we bought him his first bicycle. Steven tried to teach him how to ride it but in the process, got annoyed and impatient with John because of his inability to pick up the skills on the first lesson. It ended up with Steven spanking John, John anxious and in tears, and I, tense and upset by the whole episode. What could have been a time for fun, joy and interaction had ended up in pain.

Participating in sports with Steven was never about having fun: it was all about competition, excellence and achievement. Everything had to be done well or not at all. There was once when he told me, "If you can't play golf well at a competitive level, forget about going on the course. You're not going to have fun; the people you play with are not going to have fun; you're going to be holding up other people on the course. It's inconsiderate." What he told me affected me. It became a running tape that would reverberate in my mind, a voice that I would constantly hear to remind me to either excel at what I do or to forget about it if the best was not 'good enough.'

Steven was a hard taskmaster: a man who was never satisfied with our efforts, a man who was stingy with his approval, praise and affection. It was heart-breaking for me to discover that as much as he was critical of us in our endeavours, he thought nothing of playing golf with friends who were incompetent at the game. He would not hesitate to criticize me or to call me stupid if I happened to park the car badly, but somehow, he was quick to make allowances and excuses for his friends. He had double standards, one for his family and one for his friends. I found myself constantly having to fight him to save my selfhood, which was fast plunging into the abyss of darkness. My marriage, unfortunately, like my childhood, was fragmenting me even further.

By the time my daughter, Emily, was born, six years after my older son, John, Steven was spending more and more time away from home. He was by now reaching the pinnacle of success. The more successful he became, the more arrogant and indifferent he became towards us. The only times he would spend with us were during the weekends, mostly Sundays, as Saturdays were reserved for his golf. And even then, his main connection with us was through activities.

Steven was a man who got bored easily and family life bored him. One way he could engage with us and have fun was through outdoor activities. When he was not being competitive and pushy, we would all relax and actually have fun as a family. We would either take the children rollerblading or biking at the park, or we would go to our country club for a swim, for bowling and for their tennis lessons. We had lots of fun taking the children on short road trips to neighbouring Malaysia, where we would go hiking near the waterfalls or fishing in the rock pools. These were good times but they became less frequent as he grew busier with his work and travel.

Steven grew increasingly distant from us, often preoccupied with his work. Although we continued to travel twice a year, he was distant with us even on vacations. There was a lack of emotional bonding and intimacy in his relationship with the family. I felt frustrated and lonely, shut out from his life. He seldom spoke to me or shared with me about his work or about his life outside of the home. If I did ask, he would tell me to mind my own business, often stressing that I had nothing to do with his work. I felt as if Steven was going through the motions of doing his duty by staying with us, to show the world that he was taking care of his family. As he valued economic and social success, maintaining an image of a successful and happy family was of paramount importance to him.

Over time, Steven became the classic absentee husband and father, emotionally and physically unavailable to us. He was totally engrossed in his own life. He worked long hours, travelled frequently on business trips, entertained clients, and had a fairly active social life that excluded the children and I. He often came home late at nights and hardly saw us as we would have gone to bed by then. For a long time, I spent many lonely nights reading and listening to music after the children had gone to bed, waiting for him to return from work, longing for his companionship, but I gradually gave that up as he would often return home past midnight: I had to be up early in the morning to get the children ready for school and to get to work.

Steven practically took no interest whatsoever in our daily life, let alone our achievements. Even when he was home, he paid scant attention to us. Home was more of a hotel for him to get his clothes laundered. His continual absence from the home created more space and distance between us. Strangely, the weekends when he was home became miserable times for us. He was often edgy and irritable, and would either criticize John or myself. Not only was he unkind to me, he was also unkind to John, always picking on him for something or other, never satisfied with his efforts.

Once, when John was about 10 years old, Steven had insisted that John, who had a weight problem, get on the weighing machine at my mother's home in front of all his uncles, aunts and cousins. He insisted that John announce to everyone his weight in spite of John's pleas and my protests. Steven had thought it was funny but for John, that particular incident left a deep, traumatizing scar that John is still trying to heal. His father's lack of approval and acceptance of him has left John feeling insecure about himself despite his having conquered mild dyslexia to attain a double major in Psychology and Criminology and is in the process of completing a Master's degree. Even though physical fitness has now become a way of life for John, there are times when he grapples with body dysmorphia.

Often in those unpleasant moments, like a mother hen, I would defend John but Steven would then target me and yell at me aggressively to shut up and to stay out of it. He often made it clear, and said so in no uncertain terms, that since I was not bringing home the bacon, I had no say in any matter. Hearing him utter those words caused me great anguish and deep resentment welled up in me. I felt belittled at his lack of respect for me as a person and for my contribution to the home. I was contributing to the home in every way I could. Steven had no right to speak to me that way just because he was the main breadwinner. Men like Steven often use emotional and financial power as a way to exert control and to silence their partners.

Incidents such as this, would ignite my fury beyond measure. I would fume in silence until my seething rage would get the better of me, and then, all hell would break loose. I would explode and vent out my frustration and anger. This would escalate into nasty conflicts with ensuing shouting matches. My home was not a home in the conventional sense. It was a battleground for power with each striving to out do the other in assuming control. It was beset with tension, pain, constant fighting and misery. I could not understand why Steven had become so hostile and edgy with us, especially on the weekends. He saw so little of us. One would have presumed that he would want to spend as much time as he could with us during the weekends. But this was not the case. I noticed that his hostility towards us had worsened when he started travelling on business trips. I felt something amiss but could not fathom what it was at that time.

Steven's emotional unavailability and lack of interest in bonding with the family became a perpetual source of pain for me. I felt very much alone in this marriage, unloved and unsupported. I found myself becoming increasingly wary of trusting people with my emotions. I was angry that all my dreams and expectations of having a happy and united family and of having someone supportive in my life whom I could love and trust were not materializing in the way I had anticipated. I frequently wondered if it was ever possible to have a happy home. It seemed to me so elusive, so unimaginable, something I could only dream of. It reminded me of when I was a little girl and had craved longingly for a happy home.

And there, I believe, lies the problem of expectations going awry. Like most people, I had believed that my marriage would last forever. What I had to reconcile with was that a long, lasting and happy marriage is not a guarantee and that people do not always behave the way you expect them to. Nor do they love you the way you want them to.

To save our marriage, I had proposed that we consult a marriage counsellor but Steven would not consider it. I would try to talk with him and even write him numerous letters in my attempts to communicate the family's needs to him but he would ignore them. Sometimes, he would hear me out with a cold, bored and arrogant look on his face, swirling a glass of brandy in his hand while I spoke. When I had finished with what I had to say, he would sigh, rudely roll his eyes in an exaggerated manner, and ask me in a bored and deliberate tone, "Have you finished?"

Without looking at me further, he would get up and walk away. If I insisted on a response, he would coldly and exasperatedly ask me, "So what is it that you want? What do you want from me? Aren't the house, car and vacations enough for you? What more do you want from me? Why are you always complaining? You sound just like a broken down tape recorder, going on and on about the same thing."

I would stare at him in frustration and disbelief, furious that Steven had not cared enough to listen to what I had been saying, to consider our emotional needs, to understand that I wanted a husband and companion for myself, and a father for our children. I did not mind him working long hours if that was required of him. I had been prepared to give him the support he needed. All I wanted was love, respect, connection and communication in our home. Not this emptiness, this loneliness, the constant quarrels and criticism, nor the indifference and neglect. I wanted Steven to connect with us emotionally.

Steven often gave the excuse that he was busy and had to work late, and for a long time I believed him. Although for the most part, it may have been true, I began to wonder how he could make the time to socialize with his friends after work and not have time with his family. The lonelier I became, the more I craved his companionship, his love, just as I had craved my mother's love and touch. The more I wanted him to spend time with me, the worse it became between us.

Our marital life grew increasingly difficult and strained. When I had given up a promising full-time career for a part-time job so as to nurture my children, to look after the home-front, and to free my ex-husband from domestic obligations so that he could concentrate on his promising career, I never expected Steven, who was rising to the pinnacle of his career, to forget about me. But as he became more successful, I was conveniently pushed aside and excluded from most parts of his life. In spite of our marital difficulties, I did not imagine that

Steven would do this to me: we had gone through so many obstacles to get married, and we had shared some good times together.

I began to realize that Steven was one of those people who tended to compartmentalize their lives. He had relegated me to the domestic arena of his life, which excluded me from his public and social life. He seldom introduced me to his colleagues and friends. Nor was I invited to his official and social functions unless protocol required my presence as his spouse. Our marriage and home life assumed a mere façade for the world.

We were by now practically leading separate lives. In fact, Steven had the temerity to tell me to get on with my own life. "Look!" he said, "Don't keep waiting for me. Why don't you lead your own life, and I will lead mine. There is no need for a divorce. Just carry on with your life as it is." It was a cruel thing to say. No husband should ever tell his wife that. Deeply hurt, upset and depressed by what he had said, I continued with life as best as I could, taking care of the children and the home. It was evident that we had different expectations from the marriage.

For me, family life has always been a priority. It was sadly not so for Steven. He wanted a wife who could run his home efficiently, someone who could look after his children, stay in the background, out of his way, and not rock the boat. What he wanted was a wife to fit into the role of a housekeeper. Steven was happy to have a family as long as they remained invisible and not make demands of him.

Whenever I spoke of divorce, Steven would flatly refuse to consider it. He threatened to make life difficult for me if I ever took the children away from him. I know I should have left him a long time ago, but I did not. Not only was I afraid by his threats, my marriage had been my security blanket, and I was emotionally not ready to leave it. I was foolish and delusional in hanging on to the relationship, in secretly hoping that things between us would change some day.

Besieged with all these fears and anxieties, I found myself in a dilemma. I knew in my heart that it was a dead-end relationship: it was never going to get better, but I was afraid to get out of it. I was afraid to strike it out on my own, afraid that I would not be able to provide my children with the kind of comfort and life style that Steven could give them. I was afraid that I would be depriving them of a father and be blamed for breaking up the family unit. I was also fearful that I would be letting my children and parents down if I left the marriage.

Most of all, I was embarrassed at the failure of my marriage. I thought I was protecting all of us, especially myself, by keeping up the pretence. But little did I realize how much damage I was doing to my children and myself by staying on in an unhappy and abusive marriage. It took me time even to acknowledge to myself that I was in an abusive relationship. I was in denial. I had unwittingly done us all an injustice by not leaving the marriage, although I knew that I was going to do it at some point. I had made poor choices in my life and I was paying for them with self-betrayal and self-abandonment, invoked by a lack of self-love.

My marriage was on the rocks, but I was just too apathetic, too depressed to do anything about it. I could not summon the courage or the energy to change my circumstances. I was stuck. It was as if I was sucked into a vortex of my shadowland, unable to save myself. I was hurting so badly that at times, I felt like I was losing control of my life. I was either angry or sad most of the time. Little things could trigger me off and I would end up snapping at my children or at Steven. Feeling guilty and despising myself for my lack of self-control, I would end up crying myself to sleep, often chastising myself. Engulfed by unhappiness, my health deteriorated. Unable to eat and sleep, I began to look gaunt and tired. The dark circles under my eyes made them disappear into deep pools of sorrow. I tried to put on a brave front, especially for Emily, who craved a normal family life, but I felt dead inside.

Emily was always asking for her father. She would compare our neighbours' and her friends' families and wonder why her father never came home for dinner on weekdays and was hardly ever around to spend time with her. In her young and innocent way, she tried to understand the demands of his work but like most young children, she wanted to see more of him and craved his attention.

Given his frequent absences from home and his lack of emotional bonding with the children, it fell upon me to play the roles of both father and mother to them. It was I who took the children to the beach or to the movies on Saturdays when he went for golf. And it was I who saw to their education and to their emotional needs. Sometimes when I took my children to the beach, I would observe couples and families together and I would yearn longingly for more love and togetherness for our family. It always made me feel sad that we seldom went out for movies or meals as a family.

Even though Steven was doing well and we lived in a detached house, had two cars and a live-in domestic helper, he was often telling me to be frugal and not to waste money dining out, which was fine, as we had elaborate meals at home. But what took me by surprise was when I found out that while he was telling me to be frugal, he was entertaining others freely. When I questioned him about it, he did not deny it, and coolly replied, "Am I starving you and the children? Am I not providing for the family? Look at this," he said, waving his hands dramatically around the living room, "Isn't this a comfortable home? How many people do you think can afford to have a home like this! And don't forget, we have two vacations every year! What are you complaining about? What I do with my money is my business. It has nothing to do with you."

Steven believed that as long as he was fulfilling his responsibility by providing for the family, whatever he did in his own time had nothing to do with me. I felt angry, cheated and betrayed. Steven was cheating on me in many ways. There were telling signs of other women in his life but I would not face it for a long time. Trapped in my denial and apathy, I did nothing concrete to disprove them. Whenever I asked him if he was having an affair, he would deny it, and I would eagerly and foolishly believe him so that I could remain in my tower of denial. I wanted to believe that he was busy working every time he came home late, so I made excuses for him. Steven did not want to come right out and tell me the truth. He probably felt that as long as I did not know the truth, I would not be hurt and he could carry on with whatever he was doing.

But a wife knows when a husband is cheating on her. It is not normal for a husband to insist on leading separate lives and having separate sleeping arrangements. Unfortunately, I kept up the denial and played along with him. I would probably at that time have been totally devastated had I been confronted with his adultery. I would not have been able to live with him again. I still wanted my family to be together. I was willing to stay in that miserable and meaningless marriage, lonely and emotionally abandoned. I had put myself in a vulnerable position and I had to deal with it. So, I chose to lie to myself and to the world to save my home. The marriage was beset with dishonesty and pretence, and I, sadly played along with my fears, denial and delusion. There was nothing but lies, lies and more lies.

Chapter 6

Sadness flies on the wings of the morning and out of the heart of darkness comes light.

Jean Giraudaux

The Call of the Universe: Dream Encounter with Dark Angel

In the early hours of one morning, I woke up sweating profusely, gasping desperately for air. I had been sleeping badly over a long period of time, often getting up at odd hours, besieged with thoughts of the unhappy state of my marriage. But this particular morning, I was woken up by a dream.

I saw myself walking down a long and faintly lit, narrow hallway. There was a huge red door on my right towards the end of the passageway. Out of curiosity, I opened it and found myself peering into a dark room with elaborately designed multi-hued stained glass windows at the far end of the room. Slivers of dawn light streamed in through the windows, dancing delightfully, illuminating at once the myriad of colours, playfully mocking the shadows of the night, urging them to dispel their darkness.

Captivated by the flitting movements of the shimmering dawn light and the beckoning shadows of the night teasing one and other unceasingly, my attention was averted from them as I heard a strain of beautiful, haunting music playing in the background. I listened intently and recognized it to be one of my favourite Gregorian chants.

A sudden movement at the far end of the room startled me. I turned my gaze apprehensively towards it and noticed a large cage with a crouched figure in it. I stood there for a moment wondering what was in the cage, not daring to get any closer. Just then, a deafening, thunderous bellow startled me out of my wits. I turned towards the direction of the sound and saw a huge, dark-cloaked figure, emerging from another door on my left and approaching the cage. I stood transfixed to the spot, barely daring to breathe for fear of attracting its attention.

The dark figure was shouting menacingly at the crouched figure. I peered carefully and realized that what I thought was an animal in the cage was, in fact, a vulnerable and frightened-looking young woman. I looked at her eyes and saw deep pools of sorrow and terror in them. As the figure approached the cage, she quickly retreated to the corner, seeking comfort in the distance between them. She glanced furtively at the cloaked figure through the corner of her eyes, alert and watchful, like a fox watching its prey.

I peered at her more closely and was totally stunned when I saw her face, ever so familiar, change from that of a young woman, to that of a child, and then to a teenager, a young woman again, and finally to that of a gaunt and tired-looking middle-aged woman, all in a span of a second.

Dumbfounded, I stood there, paralyzed by the thought that I was not just the observer. I was also the observed. I gasped in horror, petrified at the realization that the frightened crouched figure in the cage was none other than me, talking to Dark Angel, the guardian of the 'Dark night of the soul.' For a moment, I wondered if I was dead. I could not fathom why was I watching myself. It was as if my 'Other' and I were one and yet separate, each subsumed by the other, riding together along the waves of self-destruction with our thoughts and emotions.

Just then I heard myself pleading with Dark Angel: "Take me a long with you. Why can't we be together? You're always going away, leaving me alone. Let's go together. We can have some time alone, won't that be nice?"

But he bellowed out a resounding "No!" interjecting at the same time, "It's not the same anymore."

"What's — not the same anymore?" I asked, nervously.

"We're not the same anymore. We're different. Things have changed between us" he retorted, irritated that I should even posit the question.

In anguish, I cried out, "Let me go my own way then. I don't want to live with you like this anymore. I can't do this anymore. I'm not happy with you. Please, let me go!"

I noticed his head tilting dangerously to one side. He stared at me in exasperation, disgust written clearly on his face.

"You just don't know how to be happy, do you? You're never satisfied. You're always complaining! You are free to go, you know! I'm not the one keeping you here. You're too weak!" He looked at me, his lips curling in contempt, "Too weak, and too frightened to leave me. Because, you know, you're not going to get anything better out there than what you have here!" He sniggered maliciously.

"You need me!" he said in a menacingly quiet tone, emphasizing each syllable with exaggeration, frightening me into desperate submission.

"Remember that! YOU NEED ME!"

And with that last retort, he stormed out of the room. I watched his retreating back in tears. Fear gripped me, debilitating fear. I was choking and trembling with emotion. There was a tightness in my chest as I felt my heart constrict dangerously. I swallowed hard. I was terrified. I had allowed myself to be charmed and seduced by Dark Angel. I had gotten into this mess and I didn't know how to get out of it.

I was plagued with uncertainties about my future: Could I make it on my own? What could I do? Where would I go? I didn't have enough money. What about my babies? What would happen to them? Would he take them away from me? I thought aloud, rocking myself back and forth, wringing my hands in desperation, terror gripping me. What if…?

Fear was obviously stopping me from walking out that door, from choosing to live the life I wanted. I felt a piercing pain in my heart. I broke down and cried bitterly. I had lost the battle. I felt trapped. I was slowly but surely succumbing to my death. My soul was dying every moment, bit by bit. There was nothing but darkness, overwhelming darkness. Sinking deeper and deeper, suffocating in the mire of misery, I gasped, choked, struggled, desperately fighting to stay alive. The more I struggled, the deeper I sank into the abysmal of darkness. Engulfed by suffocating blackness and a penetrating sense of doom, I cried out in utter despair:

"Where're you, Angel of Light? Why have you deserted me?"

I sobbed brokenly, feeling lost, alone and abandoned, not knowing what to do.

Just at that moment, I woke up from my dream with a start, breathing heavily, my chest heaving painfully with every breath, my body aching, re-living every detail of the dream. I felt overwhelmed, totally consumed by my life's experiences. I felt drained of energy and vitality. I was bone tired of fighting! I was tired of living! I was tired of life! I grieved for the death of my 'self.' What was there to look forward to, I wondered. Nothing! Only darkness! All I could see was the darkness ahead of me. No joy! No peace! No love! No light! Nothing!

It was as if the light in me had been snuffed out. I felt lost, lonely and frightened. Weary! I was weary to the bones, weighed down by my responsibilities to my family. My children needed me and I had to be there for them. I loved my children. I loved my family. I was not going to let them down despite my emptiness, my weariness, my unhappiness. So I told myself that I had to go on, at least for my children's sake!

Chapter 7

To live is the rarest thing in the world.
Most people exist, that is all.

Oscar Wilde

Disillusioned: Sucked into the Quagmire of Abuse

In spite of my determination to carry on with life as best as I could, I was desperately sinking into the pit of depression. I felt oppressed, suffocated and rejected. My self-confidence plummeted even further. I was losing every sense of my self. I was operating like a zombie, doing things mechanically, without joy.

One day, Steven's sister visited me and noticed, on her way to the washroom, that her brother was occupying another bedroom. She was shocked and shot a stream of questions at me, from wanting to know what was going on, to how long it had been going on, and if there was another woman involved. She felt quite certain that there was another woman in his life.

I told her about Steven's close relationship with his colleague and long-time companion, Jessica. They spent long hours at work, socialized outside of work and travelled on business trips together. It was obvious that they were more than good friends. The emotional bonding, communication, sharing and companionship that were evident in their relationship were sadly absent in ours.

Steven took more interest in Jessica's children and knew more about them than he did about his own children. Whenever I tried to update him on our children's progress, he would complain that I was boring, that all I talked about were the children and the home. Yet, he obviously didn't mind listening to Jessica talk about her family life. He often spoke about her children's accomplishments with a sense of pride, until one day, unable to tolerate it anymore, I told him furiously that it was not right that he should talk so much about them in front of our children and not take pride or interest in them.

If Steven paid any attention to us at all, it was more likely to be negative. Emily, however, who was more like him, extroverted in personality when she was a little girl, was seldom the target of his derision. But she was nevertheless deeply affected by her father's harsh treatment of John and myself. Deeply empathetic, she would sob her heart out, feeling intensely our pain each time he targeted us. Terrified that she would also receive the same treatment from her father if she did not meet his high standards or comply with his wishes, Emily developed perfectionistic tendencies in her constant striving to achieve excellence.

Having witnessed many of our quarrels and some of Steven's physical abuse, the trauma Emily sustained as a child, unfortunately, manifested as nervous tension that developed further into migraine, chronic fatigue and fibromyalgia. John too, affected by the tension and unhappiness in the home, displayed signs of depression and sought food as his comfort and, in the process, gained much weight, much to the derision of his father.

As much as I knew I had to leave the marriage for myself and for my children's sake, I struggled with the decision. The thought of leaving Steven evoked in me deep pangs of separation anxiety. Overwhelmed by fear, I often felt like a tormented fish out of water, struggling and trashing wildly in the throes of excruciating pain. Sad and lonely, I began to internalize the pain as I had done as a child.

In the of pangs of Steven's rejection, wounded and fragmented by his abusive name-calling and emotional neglect, I found myself experiencing a whole gamut of conflicting emotions: from deep sadness, to fuming silence and resentment, to striking out like a spiteful cat in fury, fighting him every inch of the way if he so much as criticized us. I became increasingly defensive by the day, fuelled by a dire need to be constantly on my guard to protect myself from the onslaught of his verbal attacks. I was turning into someone I could not recognize; I was irritable, angry and bitter. To protect myself, I assumed a wall of hard veneer, finding safety in it.

I often felt like a volcano, waiting to erupt without much provocation from the pent up frustration and anger, repressed over the years because I had unwisely chosen not to seek help, not even a listening ear. Having no desire to wash dirty linen in public or to tarnish Steven's public image, I conscientiously kept everything that had happened in our marriage a secret from my family and friends. But most of all, I had no desire to divulge that my home was as volatile and disruptive as a volcano; its inhabitants, waiting to spew out torrents of mutual abuse.

I knew that the animosity between us had to stop at some point. I could not cope with the pain anymore. It was unbearable. It was tearing me apart. It was tearing my children apart. It was tearing apart our home. Scorched by this burning ball of fire that was threatening to consume us into total oblivion, I knew I had to take action to extinguish it before it completely destroyed us.

As I sat by the beach watching the sun set, reflecting on my life and the course of action I planned to take, I felt certain that God would want me to take the alternative route. By doing so, I would be honouring the sacredness of life. Although keeping the family together and the marriage intact were of paramount importance to me, I wondered at the cost. Neither my children nor I deserved to be treated with disregard and indifference. I would be perpetuating the cycle of abuse by doing nothing about it. I thought of another dream I had the night before; it was another wake-up call from the universe, just like my dream about Dark Angel.

I dreamt that I was standing in my bathtub with a newborn baby in my hands. As I stooped down to wash its hair, I fell into a deep slumber. The next moment, I woke up with a start, glanced at the baby in my arms, and screamed hysterically. The baby was still; it had turned blue. I cried out in horror, realizing immediately that I had somehow submerged the baby in the water.

I stared at it for a moment, sobbing loudly, rocking it to and fro, as if the very action would revive it. I came quickly to my senses and frantically tried to resuscitate it. I screamed desperately for Steven to help me save the baby. But he was not there. I was alone, standing in the bathtub with the baby in my arms. There was nothing I could do to save it. I had killed the baby. I was shivering and crying out desperately, over and over again, that I had killed the baby. I had killed the baby! I woke up crying in my sleep, distressed and deeply shocked, overcome by an unbearable gnawing pain, a pain that remained with me over the next few days.

I thought about the dream all of the next day. I was disturbed and shaken by its significance to my life. I could still feel the palpable emptiness that had struck me like a blow, deep in my womb, as if I had deliberately aborted the baby. I told my closest friend, Rina, about it. She stared at me coolly and replied without batting an eyelid, "You do realize, of course, that the baby is you! You've allowed your inner child to die!"

As I sat, reflecting on what she had said and its significance to my life, I knew it was true. The universe was revealing to me through my dreams what I had refused to acknowledge: aspects of my life that needed attention and change. I had allowed my inner child to die: I was not living my life; I had merely existed. I had become nothing but a walking zombie: lifeless and joyless.

Chapter 8

In the night of the Soul, bright flows the river of God.

George Santayana

Fate Takes a Turn For The Worse: Standing by Steven

I had made up the decision to leave the marriage and was looking into the possibility of immigrating when fate took a turn for the worse. I found myself having to stand by Steven, whose booming business took a hard hit in the global economic collapse. Many of his overseas offices had to be shut down, employees terminated and assets sold off to pay off outstanding loans and staff's salaries. We were faced with the reality of bankruptcy and feared losing our home. It was a gruelling period for all of us, emotionally and financially. Steven, who was once an atheist, found solace in God. There was a softness to him now that paved the way for more communication between us.

Despite this improvement in our relationship, Steven's overly-close relationship with Jessica continued to be the bane of my happiness. Steven had always openly acknowledged Jessica as his best friend and I presume he felt grateful to have her stand by him during trying times at work. This was yet another opportunity for her to prove her loyalty to him. I had once accepted their friendship as normal in the early years of their relationship as I had thought it natural that they should be close, given the hours they spent working together.

I had foolishly disregarded the rumours about them, until one day, when Jessica came over to my home, presumably to discuss work, I noticed then how Steven's eyes lit up the minute he saw her. Despite the fact that he saw her almost every day at work and outside of work, the eagerness, excitement and animation he displayed on seeing her was so unlike the coolness with which he greeted me, even after his long business trips. I sensed that the already deep and strong bond between the two of them was even stronger now with this trial. Steven doted on her and did not bother to conceal the fact. He was protective and defensive when it came to her. It became increasingly evident to me that they were emotionally dependent on each other and were more than good friends.

During this period, to lighten the overwhelm we were enduring, my daughter Emily and I decided to plan a small birthday party for him with family members and some close friends. In spite of knowing how I felt about Jessica, Steven still insisted on having her at the party. When I refused, he told me in a quiet and steady tone, "She means a lot to me. If she is not going to be invited, then I would rather not have the party." My heart sank as I heard those words. I felt the now familiar, deep-wrenching pain in my heart at his rejection. I was hurt and so was Emily that he had not bothered to consider our feelings.

As much as I tried to be cordial to Jessica on those occasions when we did meet, it always proved painful for me to witness their obvious closeness and affection for each other. There was once when I told Steven that he could not carry on blatantly displaying his affection for his companion in my presence and that I did not want him to visit her at her home, nor be seen having meals with her and her children in public, he replied, "You have no right to make me choose between a close friend and family. If you force me to make a choice then I will choose to divorce you."

Steven had shown me no respect and consideration throughout our marriage and had taken me for granted because he had believed that I would never leave him; that I would somehow always tolerate his indiscretions despite our constant conflicts. The marriage had left me feeling totally weary and dead inside. It became unbearable and impossible for me to live with him in the same house even though we were living separate lives. I prayed fervently for God to deliver both of us, to free him from this trial and to free me from this bondage. I continued to stand by him, painful as it was for both of us until I had ascertained that Steven was no longer in danger of bankruptcy. I kept reminding myself during this whole period of what my father had once said, "You never leave your partner in fire."

As soon as we could, Emily and I made the move to Canada to join John, who was already living in Toronto. As for Steven, he is now back on his feet. I am confident that he will, in a matter of time, rise to the top again in his career. He is a very capable, conscientious and intelligent man and work has always been his first priority in life, so I believe there is no reason for him not to be successful. With God's grace and love, my anger and bitterness have been slowly dissipating. I believe that when we leave our failed relationships with peace and love rather than with hatred and recrimination, it is more likely to end amicably than acrimoniously. That is my intention: after all, we share the same children.

Chapter 9

*When I called, you answered me. You
made me bold and stouthearted.*

Psalm 138

Moving Forward: Embracing the Flame of Hope

As I embraced the flame of hope in my heart, I went through a shift in consciousness. Where once, I had been unable to break away emotionally from Steven, now I was, with God's grace, love and strength, able to detach myself emotionally from him. I knew that I could live without him, without experiencing the emptiness, anxiety and heart-wrenching pain of separating from someone whom I have known since a teenager.

Time is what I need, I reassured myself, to heal and to claim back my power that I had given away in this dysfunctional relationship. It had inflicted inexplicable emotional and psychological damage to my children and myself. With a new sense of clarity, I begun to acknowledge openly that I had not loved and honoured myself. I had lived in fear, in denial, and self-deception because it had been easier to live a lie than to face the reality of my situation, to confront my fears and anxieties. I had allowed myself to drown in the dark and murky waters that had obliterated the light in me. I had failed to honour the sacredness of life!

My journey to healing began when I finally acceded to my soul's nudgings to move forward to honour life. It compelled me to turn inward to look honestly within myself, to reassess my situation and to acknowledge and accept its reality. In the process, I had to let go of self-denial and self-deception. I had to confront the inner demons that were keeping me anchored in my deep-rooted fears and anxieties. I also had to surrender my victim consciousness by acknowledging to myself that I, and only I, was responsible for the quality of my life and no one else.

I have traversed the dark and lonely path of hurt, anger, bitterness, depression and grief, wounded and fragmented by my life's experiences. But now I remind myself that the grief and the non-acceptance of what had transpired in my life will only keep me imprisoned and bound to my past if I do not release them and surrender to the present moment. I cannot alter the events that have occurred in my past, but I can certainly change what I do not want in my life now.

Abuse, as I have come to learn, can only take place if we allow ourselves to be taken advantage of and treated in unacceptable ways. People tend to treat you the way you treat yourself. I have become more conscious now of what I will tolerate and not tolerate in my interactions with others. In other words, I am learning to lay down appropriate boundaries that will not compromise my selfhood.

As I work on myself daily with the help of God's grace, I am gaining the strength and courage to do what is best for me. I am learning to make myself a priority and to take the time to do the things I want to do with my life. I know I have to make myself happy and not depend on another person to fulfil me as I had done with Steven. I have to find the peace and joy within me first before I can make others around me happy. It is up to me to seek and walk my truth even if that truth does not comply with the truth of others. Only then, I know, can I be free from approval-seeking behaviours.

My healing journey has made me notice that issues that I had once refused to deal with kept resurfacing in my relationships in order for me to heal. Until we resolve our issues, they will continue to keep us in fetters and we will keep perpetuating old patterns of behaviour, remaining stuck in the quicksand of suffering. The road to growth and empowerment lies within each and every one of us but unless we learn to love ourselves first and acknowledge our worthiness, we will be unable to break free from the shackles of our own making, as I am learning every day.

I have faith and trust that God is leading me to where I am supposed to go and what I am supposed to do. I believe, like everyone else, I am here for a reason. I believe that we all choose the life we want, consciously or unconsciously. I had unwittingly accepted the reality of abuse and so had participated in perpetuating its cycle. My life is what I have made of it and I acknowledge that I am where I am today because of the choices I made yesterday. I am not making excuses for the perpetrators of abuse but I strongly believe that we must, as victims of abuse, who can ourselves become perpetrators of abuse in our bitterness, take responsibility for our lives by not perpetuating it any further with our anger, hatred, retaliation and revenge.

Albert Einstein once said, "There are two ways to live your life. One is as though nothing is a miracle. The other is as though everything is." I have decided to choose the latter, that life is a miracle, a cycle of creation in our hands and that it is entirely up to us to manifest the kind of life that we want. I strongly believe now that nothing in life is impossible when we have God with us and in us.

As I grow stronger in my spiritual walk, I know that only forgiveness can liberate us from what has transpired in our lives; only forgiveness can free us from our suffering, and help us to move forward to lead new lives. I know that I have to start by forgiving myself first, and not disempower myself daily with self-remorse and guilt. I am not going to lie to myself that forgiving myself and the people who have hurt me is going to be an easy task or that it would happen overnight but I am determined to release myself from this bondage that keeps me tied to past memories and unhappiness.

With the decision to move on and save myself from drowning even further, I have reached for the light, the light that has made me choose life. What I want others in my situation to know is that no matter how long it takes, we can start over again, we can choose again. We can make a better choice for ourselves. And in doing so, we liberate ourselves.

The flame of hope, like the flowers of the Flame of the Forest tree, burns deep in my heart, igniting me forward to live my life fully, to fulfil my purpose and God's will for me. I look forward to a new life, in a new land, with new possibilities. I see myself leaving the dark and gloomy winter season of my life and entering the spring season with excitement, yet with some trepidation, as I do not know what life has to offer me. All I know is that there is always good and bad in life; the polarities are inescapable. It is how we engage with life and how we view and overcome our obstacles and challenges along our life's journey that matter most.

I can only trust that our Creator, who has been guiding me, will continue to guide me to better things. I live my life with gratitude for my family, for all the people in my life who have provided me with love and support along my journey, gratitude for my blessings, and even for my ex-husband, who has been my greatest teacher of all. I have come to view my life as experiences that could have been better had I been more conscious of exercising better choices.

As I take a deep breath of the fresh sea air, the noon sun now beating down strongly on my shoulders, I glance around and remind myself of how wonderful it is to choose life and to be given a second chance! I know deep within me that would be what God would want me to do, to move on and to grasp life, for better or for worse. As clichéd as it may sound, life must go on!

Chapter 10

Above all things let us never forget that mankind constitutes one great brotherhood; all born to encounter suffering and sorrow, and therefore bound to sympathize with each other.

Albert Pike

Miriam: A Kindred Soul in Distress

I met Miriam, a 32-year-old insurance agent, at a yoga retreat at Desaru, Malaysia. I was drawn to her quiet air of serenity and to her dark brown, soulful eyes that had an amazing intensity to them when she looked at you unflinchingly in the eye. There was a sweet gentleness to her smile and yet I could detect a subtle wryness in the curl of her lips. We got along well, right from the beginning, each drawn to the other with the recognition of kindred spirits.

That evening, after dinner, we took a walk along the beach to the beach bar, chatting inanely about almost everything under the sun. One topic led to another and then to our families. There was a comfortable silence between us as we listened to the waves and sipped wine, each revelling in our own stillness. I opened up to her first and shared with her my marital woes. I told her that I was writing a book on abuse and betrayal and that I wanted to share my story with others.

Miriam listened intently, asked me more about the book, ran a quick appraisal over me as I spoke, and then glanced away in silence to watch the waves. Then she turned around, looked directly into my eyes with those piercing eyes of hers and poured out everything about her life: how she had suffered the humiliation of sexual abuse at the hands of her ex-husband, who she had met at the age of 20, had divorced him after much struggle, and was now a successful insurance agent living alone with her two boys and a live-in domestic helper.

It was as if a dam had been broken in her as she let loose an avalanche of emotions that had long been repressed. But even as she spoke, Miriam maintained her dignity with a stillness that I have come to respect and admire in that short span of time. Beneath the quiet assurance and the steeliness in her voice, which belied her gentle demeanour and petite figure, I could discern a tinge of sadness. As Miriam laid bare her life's story, I felt myself drawn into her life, experiencing her deep pain and hurt.

In the early years of her marriage, Miriam submitted to her ex-husband's kinky sexual exploits and demands, allowing him to manipulate her into believing that if she truly loved him, she would not hesitate to make him happy and comply with his demands. In a voice constricted with pain, Miriam recounted sadly:

"I was often besieged with feelings of guilt and shame. I submitted to his demands because I thought, you know, when you love someone, it seems like the right and caring thing to do. Yet, in my heart, I was not happy. It didn't feel right. I felt like I was compromising my values. Can you believe it? He even wanted me to have sex with his friend. He said that the thought of me with another man excited him; if he could watch me having sex with other men, it would be even better. When I heard that, I decided that it was time to put my foot down. I was shocked with his proposition. I didn't believe in open relationships and still don't. It's not my style. It would violate my dignity—my rights, my beliefs. It was bad enough that I was undermining myself, succumbing to his sexual demands. I wasn't going to sleep with other men just to excite my husband."

Miriam said that as his demands for more kinky sex increased and violated her sense of self, she began to protest and refused to submit to him. This made him furious. He would hurl abuse at her and occasionally rape her. It made her feel tainted and ugly, and a seething rage and hatred welled up in her. Miriam began to see him for who he was: a spoiled, self-absorbed sexual pervert who was consumed by his primal, lustful instincts. His excessive indulgence in sexual fantasy and pornography repulsed her.

Often, Miriam said, he would come home late at night, reeking of alcohol and take her by force. Afraid of his wrath and violence, she would submit to his unrelenting lust. She felt angry, used, morally degraded and defeated. From a lively and bubbly person, Miriam, who had become beaten and downtrodden, grew increasingly silent and withdrawn, her spirit, broken.

Financially dependent on her husband, having given up her work when the children were born, Miriam felt helpless, not having money of her own. Her husband controlled the purse strings and would dole out only sufficient money for the household. As the children attended school and had extra classes, she found it difficult to manage with the money he gave her. To supplement the household income, she decided to tutor students at home.

Miriam suspected that he had more money than he gave her. Sometimes, he would be generous and would give her more, but at other times, he would hold back money until she had to ask him for it. She felt upset, frustrated and embarrassed that he should belittle her into asking him for money. It was, she believed, his way of keeping her in check and establishing control over her.

Despite her misery, Miriam felt too ashamed to seek help, especially from her family and friends. Feeling alone and depressed, she began to avoid contact with people. She felt she could not possibly talk to anyone about her situation. "How can I tell my family and friends that my husband is a sexual pervert, a philanderer, that my husband forces me to watch pornography with him and wants me to perform indecent acts? How can I tell them that he rapes me, that he wants me to have sex with other men?" she asked in distress, tears rolling down her face. I listened in silence, distraught.

Although, Miriam was desperate to leave her husband, she was afraid. She had no money, but more than that, she was terrified of what he would do to her if she took the children and left. She feared for her life. He had threatened to hurt her if she ever left him and took their children with her. Besides, he had said that he would not support the children, and she knew that it would be difficult for her without his financial support. So she continued living with him, feeling alone and miserable.

Given his insatiable sexual appetite, Miriam knew that he would not be content to be with her in a monogamous relationship. She suspected he was having affairs when she detected wafts of women's perfume on his shirt when he came home late at nights. She had also seen him include casual clothes that were more appropriate for a vacation when he packed luggage for business trips. She suspected that he was probably extending his work trips or incorporating pleasure with work. Miriam was relieved to have him out of the house and away from her.

Once, Miriam had picked up a phone call from a woman who had mistakenly called her husband on his residential line. Caught by surprise when Miriam answered the phone, the woman had hesitated for a moment, started to say something to Miriam but quickly changed her mind and hung up. When Miriam mentioned the phone call to her husband, he laughed cruelly at her and said, "What do you expect? You're frigid—and a bore. You don't even offer me good sex. She does. She's one hot babe; she does things to me that I like."

Miriam's husband gleefully announced to her once that should any woman throw herself at him, he would be stupid to refuse her offer. His cruelty knew no bounds when he began to taunt her about her small breasts, which he said were so unlike those of his girlfriend's. He told her in a mocking tone that he was having more fun with other women than he ever did with her. Amused by her consternation, he attempted to justify his actions, coolly saying: "Do you expect me not to be bored, sleeping with the same person, having the same body, night after night, for more than 12 years?" As she mouthed his words slowly, gazing towards the sea with unseeing eyes, I could feel her pain, her feelings of rejection. Miriam's husband even had the temerity to tell her to lighten up, that it was fun to have other partners, and that she should perhaps share her love with others as he was doing.

Miriam felt trapped by her situation. Depressed and lonely, she thought of her children, her deep and abiding love for them, the treasures of her heart. Like me, she too wondered if she could provide for them as well as he could if she left the marriage. Her husband was a good provider but he was impersonal and somewhat indifferent to the emotional needs of his family, often wrapped up in his own world, work and social life. Most of the time, like my ex-husband Steven, Miriam said that her husband ignored her. The only time he interacted with her, if at all, was if he wanted the occasional sex (he left her alone most times now), and at family gatherings when both of them would conveniently play out their roles, keeping up the façade so that no one would suspect that anything was amiss in their marriage.

Besides that, he was never there for her. Miriam was very much alone in her marriage as I had been. She did not have many friends, nor would she have confided in them anyway, she said. She valued her privacy and was determined to maintain her dignity with the outside world. She played her part so well that nobody, not even her family members, knew the depth of her marital problems. She suspected that her closest friend, Lara, who had sensed her unhappiness, had hinted several times that she would be there for her if Miriam wanted to open up and talk to her. But foolish pride, she said, had stopped her from seeking help, to her detriment.

This state of affairs continued for several years, until one afternoon as she sat in the sanctuary at her church, seeking solace, praying and crying out her distress to God, she felt the Lord speak to her. Overwhelmed with emotion, Miriam sobbed desperately, crying out for help. As she sat there praying, she felt a surge of inner strength course through her body, awakening in her the realization that nothing was insurmountable; that she, Miriam, could take control of her life, and do something about her situation. She was tired of pretending, she was tired of complying with societal propriety and familial expectations. She was desperate to get out of the marriage.

In a moment of despairing self-recrimination, Miriam asked herself what she was doing with the life that God had given her. Why was she allowing this man to control her life; why was she submitting herself to abuse, criticism, put downs and contempt? Why was she punishing herself, staying in a relationship that was humiliating her and eating into her very self-esteem and self-love?

Miriam knew that she was destroying herself and her children with all the negative emotion, subjecting them to unnecessary misery. Her children were unhappy: they were badly affected by the perpetual fights and with seeing her depressed and miserable. They too, like my children, missed having a loving father, a father who would take an interest in them and love and accept them for themselves.

Miriam realized that she was still young and could start life afresh. As she sat and prayed, she felt a compelling need to break away from this bondage while she had the courage to do so. She knew that she owed it to herself and to her children to leave the marriage. The weariness, depression and apathy that had long been a part of her life were slowly giving way to an empowering realization that she had to take action to help herself, that it was entirely up to her to make the changes and that she was really not without any choice as she had once believed.

But Miriam knew that she couldn't do it alone: she needed help. She admitted to herself that she was terrified at the prospect of leaving the marriage, her comfort zone, in spite of her intolerable situation. Having lost her confidence and self-esteem, the thought of venturing out into the working world again terrified her. But she knew that she had to do it, she had to make a choice. She could not go on living with a man who had shown her no love and respect, who had humiliated her and had been cruel to her. She recognized the truth that she had been nothing more than a possession to him, an instrument to meet his physical needs. As she continued to pray, thinking about what to do with her life, she remembered seeing an article in a magazine that had listed a number of organizations she could turn to for help. Miriam felt an urgent need tugging at her heart to take the first step to help herself by seeking assistance.

The minute she got home from church, she went through the pile of magazines stored away in her closet until she found the one she was looking for. There were a number of telephone numbers but she chose to call up AWARE, a woman's organization in Singapore that helped abused and battered women. She spoke with a crisis volunteer and felt an overwhelming sense of relief in unburdening herself to someone who could understand her predicament.

Over the next few months, Miriam received a great deal of help and encouragement from the organization. They set up several appointments for her with a volunteer lawyer. On her part, she spent her time at their library, reading up on the Women's Charter, to find out about her rights in a divorce. As part of the healing process, they linked her and her children up with a professional counsellor to deal with the emotional trauma they had sustained. With the support of the women in the organization, the church, friends and her family, Miriam summoned the courage and strength to walk out of her marital home while her husband was out-station. She took her children, armed herself with a Restraining Order and went to live with her mother while she filed for divorce. The day she walked out of her marital home, she said that she felt like a caged bird that had been finally set free. She felt liberated and excited at the prospect of once again being in control of her life.

With the money her sister had loaned her, Miriam enrolled in an insurance course and found a job while her mother took care of her children. She worked diligently, spent quality time with her children, took up short courses to upgrade herself, and worked her way up to becoming a successful insurance agent. After three years of hard work and persistence, she begun to reap the rewards and made good money. She had invested money in insurance for herself and her children. With her success increasing phenomenally, she turned her attention to helping others, especially abused women and children.

She feels that as she has been blessed with abundance, it is now her turn to return to society, to help those in need.

Much of her spare time now is devoted to spending time with her children and helping to implement financial training programs at women's organizations, to help women, especially those from the lower income groups, to empower themselves financially. Miriam knows from her experience of being a vulnerable homemaker who had depended on her husband financially that it is imperative that women learn to be not only emotionally but also economically independent. It would give them, she stresses, the confidence and the bargaining power to negotiate, especially in a relationship that uses money and control to submit the non-working partner to silent dependence and denigration.

Although some of the emotional scars sustained from her abusive marriage still remain, Miriam was determined to move forward. I looked at her as she spoke, wondering in amazement at her strength and the love in her heart. Here was a wonderful woman any man would be fortunate to have, and yet her ex-husband had not appreciated and valued her. Right now, Miriam is taking the time to enjoy life with her children and friends, to travel and to grow in her spiritual path. Although she has just started going out on casual dates, she is quick to point out that she is not ready for a serious commitment. I could understand that, having gone through such an experience myself. I look at her fondly and feel honoured that this private woman could trust me enough to open her heart to me and to share her story.

Chapter 11

The greatest tragedy in life is not that men perish, but that they cease to love.

W. Somerset Maugham

Jasareen and Tessa: Abuse Knows No Boundaries

A couple of weeks after our first meeting at Desaru, I called up Miriam on the phone for a chat. She was delighted to hear from me. We chatted easily for a while, like old friends. Miriam suggested that I meet two other women whom she had befriended at AWARE, who had undergone similar experiences as us. She had told them about me and the book that I was writing. They had agreed to share their experiences with me. Like me, they too had felt that it was important for us to share our experiences with those in similar circumstances. By sharing our stories of how we transcended our predicament, we want others to know that there is safety in moving forward, in making better choices for oneself. So we gladly arranged to meet the following Saturday at Miriam's place for lunch.

Saturday arrived. I got myself ready, equipped myself with a tape recorder and drove to Miriam's home. I arrived a little early as I thought I would give her a helping hand with the food. Her domestic helper however had prepared and laid out a simple lunch on a white-laced table cloth. I handed her the tiramisu dessert I had prepared the night before and proceeded to the living room to wait for Miriam.

She had a lovely, cozy apartment that was well decorated with some fine pieces of art and souvenir from her travels. She obviously had an eye for detail. Five minutes later, Miriam emerged from her bedroom, immaculately dressed in a pristine white sundress, her hair tied up smartly in a chignon. It was good to see her again. She greeted me with much warmth; I was touched. We chatted and had a glass of white wine while we waited for the other two women to arrive.

Soon, I was being introduced to Jasareen, an American woman, working in Singapore as nanny to the children of an American couple, and Tessa, an Austrian, who was a professor in Philosophy at one of the local universities. They were smartly dressed, well-educated and interesting. After our simple but delectable lunch, I ventured to ask Jasareen what had brought her to Singapore.

Jasareen was eager to talk. She looked at me with her steady blue eyes, and without any hesitation, told me that it had all started when, at the age of 26, she had developed a burning desire to see the world outside of America. Having grown up in a small town in Oregon and having worked as a waitress for three years after completing high school, Jasareen, discontented with her provincial lifestyle, became consumed by this desire to expand her horizon, to experience life beyond where she was living. She craved adventure and excitement.

One day, while she was scanning through the newspaper, she spotted an advertisement for a nanny to accompany an American couple with two children from Seattle on a job posting to Australia for two years. She knew this was it. The opportunity had arrived at the opportune time to assuage her restlessness and desire to experience something more.

Excited at the thought of venturing out into new pastures, Jasareen made an appointment, and went for the interview. She was single, had a high school education and was bursting with energy. Although there were other applicants, Jasareen's vivacious personality and warmth won her the job. She was required to look after two children, a girl of nine and a boy of six. As her employers were required to travel and entertain as part of their job scope, she was to be responsible for the children whenever they were called away on official duty.

In Jasareen's Words:

"We arrived in Melbourne in the summer of 2005, greatly excited by the anticipation of living in Australia. I soon settled down happily to life with the Robertsons. The room I was given was tastefully furnished, with a panoramic view of the sea. The children were great kids; we got along well and did fun things together. I supervised their homework and accompanied them to their extra-curricula classes. I saw much of Melbourne and the other cities of Australia with the Robertsons. I couldn't believe my good fortune. Getting the job was the best thing that had happened to me; it was allowing me to see and experience so much of another country. Everything was new and exciting.

"On my days off, I would spend my time either relaxing at the beach or window-shopping in the city, often sitting at cafes, reading and watching the world go by. The world was opening up for me and I was eager to grasp every opportunity to savour the new sights, sounds and smells. Life was wonderful and I was deliriously happy! This was exactly what I had been yearning for.

"During one of my regular sojourns to the beach, I met Michael, a divorcee with three daughters. A rather good-looking man, tall and debonair, the kind of man most women would fall for, I found Michael irresistible and was soon falling head over heels in love with him. He captivated my heart like none of my former boyfriends had ever done. He made me laugh. He was funny, witty and interesting, always having a story at hand to render. We could talk about almost everything under the sun. I felt gloriously happy and light-hearted whenever I was with him.

"After six months of romancing, Michael proposed. I was ecstatic. I couldn't believe my life was turning out so well. Without further thought, I quit my well-paying job with the Robertsons, staying only for another month and a half for them to find a replacement, and then married Michael in a simple ceremony attended by his children and a couple of Michael's friends and family. Never would I have imagined that my life would one day turn into a nightmare.

"Michael and I drove out to Torquay, a holiday resort town in Victoria, a city south of Australia, for a week for our honeymoon while his children went off to stay with their mother. Michael did not like to leave them with her as he complained that she was an alcoholic and would not take good care of them.

"We had a wonderful and most memorable time on our honeymoon, swimming and basking in the sun, eating seafood and drinking lots of beer and wine. It was glorious; I was madly in love with Michael and I didn't want it to end. Michael behaved the perfect gentleman, attentive, considerate and very loving all throughout the honeymoon. But, all too soon, our honeymoon was over.

"When we returned home, I immediately took over the household chores and assumed the role of caregiver to his three daughters. Although I had been prepared to face some resistance from his children as I knew that it would be difficult for them to have a stranger in their home, let alone, accept me as a step-mom, I had not expected to face such open hostility from them. I was good with children and I thought it would be just a matter of time before I would win them over.

"But I was mistaken. Michael's daughters, who were eight, 12 and 14, gave me a rough time from the beginning. They were determined to make my life miserable. They resented my presence in their home and were either extremely rude to me or ignored me. They mocked my American accent, unceasingly complained about the food I prepared, threw their clothes, shoes and books all over the place and expected me to clean up after them. I was frustrated with their bad behaviour. Whenever, I insisted that they take responsibility and clean up their mess, they would scream and hurl uncalled for expletives at me. With condescension in their tone, they would ask me what I was there for.

"To my surprise, Michael did nothing to reprimand them. In fact, when I insisted that he speak to them about the way they treated me, he brusquely and unsympathetically announced that I was to cope with it, and that it was my duty as a stepmother to learn how to handle his daughters and to run the home. He reiterated emphatically that he despised hearing me complain about his children. I was astonished to hear the harshness in his tone. I felt something amiss. This was not the man I had married. This was a side of him I had not seen when we were dating.

"As the weeks and months passed by, Michael ceased to be the attentive, funny and light-hearted person that he had been when I first met him. He would either flop on the sofa in front of the television when he came home from work or he would be out drinking at the pubs with his buddies and come home drunk. The days when he stayed home, he would ignore me. If I tried to engage him in conversation, Michael would either give me monosyllabic answers that left me feeling even more frustrated or he would ignore me, show his irritation and annoyance at being disturbed.

"I was frustrated, lonely, tired and hurt. I had to prepare the girls' breakfast and lunch, send them off to school, do the laundry, pick up groceries, pay the bills and make sure that dinner was ready by the time Michael and the children returned home in the evening. Michael's aloofness made me wonder if he had married me so that I could be his unpaid housekeeper. I felt used and unappreciated. I began to nurse a deep resentment, wondering at my stupidity and hastiness in rushing into marriage with a man I had come to realize too late that I hardly knew.

"One evening, about six months into our marriage, Michael complained about the household expenses and urged me to take on a job to help out. Michael worked as a building contractor and did not bring home much income. I was eager to get out of the house and to earn my own money. I had always been financially independent and had enjoyed having money of my own. I jumped at the opportunity to get out of the house and got a part-time job as a salesperson at a department store in the city.

"I made some friends and was generally happy at work but I dreaded going home after work. I did not look forward to the endless chores and chaos awaiting me, and the daily drudgery I faced at home. I was constantly on my feet, working my butt off for this family and yet there was not even an ounce of appreciation from any one of them. I was exhausted and miserable. All I seemed to be doing was to work, work, and work. I did not have any free time for myself and became increasingly resentful. When I requested that Michael chip in with the household chores since it was his children, he became angry and turned abusive. He yelled at me and said that running the home was my job, not his.

"We were soon quarrelling over money and chores. The first month I brought home my first pay check, Michael demanded that I hand over my earnings to him and when I refused, he hit me, pushed me aside and took the money from my wallet, laughing at my attempts to stop him. Over the next two months, Michael became more abusive and violent, often swearing at me when drunk. Once, when I threatened to leave him, Michael looked at me with a glint in his eyes and said in a dangerously quiet tone, 'Don't you dare walk out on me, I'll kill you. I'll bash you up so bad, you'll never see the daylight again.'

"I was terrified. Something was telling me that he meant what he had said. I had to somehow get away from him before something drastic happened to me. I was depressed and felt unable to protect myself, unable to get out of this mess, when I knew I should.

"Then one night, as I was preparing for bed, I caught Michael stealing from my wallet again. Something snapped in me and I shouted at him furiously. 'How dare you take my money without asking me! I'm sick and tired of you and your children. What do you think I am, a bimbo? I'm not going to stand for you hitting and bullying me anymore! I'm not your slave! I didn't marry you to be your slave. I've had it with you! I'm leaving!'

"At first, Michael did not say a word. There was a pregnant silence. I could hear myself breathing rapidly. I looked at him and noticed the dangerous glint in his eyes. My stomach knotted instantly in fear. I knew what was coming; I had to get out of the room quickly. Michael looked at me with a steady and furious gaze, and the very next moment, as I tried to run out of the room, screaming in terror, I saw

Michael through the corner of my eyes, swinging his fist towards me, shouting in a rage, 'I'll kill you! You think you can get away from me, you bitch! You're never going to leave me.'

"Before I could duck, I felt an excruciating pain in my head. I had received a splitting blow to the left side of it. I staggered and then, I felt another blow, and another rain down on me, one after another. He was like a hawk tenaciously gripping its prey for the kill. An agonizing, burning pain surged through my jaw and skull. I reeled backwards, hitting my head on the corner of the table. I was in total shock. The pain was unbelievable! It was excruciating! I cried out in horror.

"All I could hear was this droning, deafening sound buzzing in my left ear. I could not hear or see anything. My vision was blurred. Pain, excruciating pain, seared through my whole body and head. I thought I was going to die. There was a lot of blood oozing from my head. I felt it sticky and wet, running down my neck, soaking my white floral blouse. I lay stunned on the floor, unable to move. I summoned what little strength I had left, heaving heavily on my arms to get up. For a moment, the whole room spun dangerously in front of me, and then, there was nothing but total blackness.

"By the time I regained consciousness, I found myself in the hospital. My head was bandaged. I had suffered deep gaping cuts to my head that needed stitches, my left ear drum was bust, and my jaw broken. I sobbed when I saw myself in the mirror. My face was completely swollen and bruised. It was unrecognizable. I knew that it would be quite a while before the wounds healed, physically and emotionally. I felt lost, alone, unloved, and unwanted. Like a bird with clipped wings, I was broken in body and spirit.

"The police came to take statements from me. They asked me if I had any family in Australia, and I said no, no one at all. I had no desire to contact my family in Oregon. I did not want to tell them what had happened. Neither did I want to return to America, not yet any way and definitely not this way. I had left Oregon with such high hopes and excitement, and now, because of a bad and hasty choice, I was totally broken.

"I thought of my ex-employers, with whom I had remained in contact and decided to contact them. They had moved to Singapore on another posting. I called them up and told them what had transpired. I told them that I was in dire need of a job and asked them if they could help me out by getting me a job in Singapore. They were shocked by my news and promised to help me.

"I stayed at the hospital for a couple of months, and then went to a friend's house to recuperate for another three weeks before I left for Singapore. I had to have a hearing aid fitted in my ear as I had lost hearing in my left ear. The doctors fixed my jaw. Metal plates were inserted to help heal the broken bone and to keep it aligned. A part of the hospital charges were taken care of by my ex-employers and the other part by the Australian social welfare. I filed for divorce as soon as I could. I was advised to proceed with charges against Michael. I did not want to stay any longer than I had to in Australia and if I did go ahead with the charges, I would have had to either remain in Australia or return at a later date for the court hearing. I was desperate to get out of the country as soon as possible and to close this chapter of my life so I declined to press charges. Michael however was jailed for a month for domestic violence that had almost caused me my life."

There was silence as Jasareen came to the end of her story, her eyes wet with tears. We were shocked and rendered speechless at the extent of her suffering. It was as if in that moment, we were 'one' in experiencing her broken spirit, her pain and hurt coursing through every single nerve and fibre in our own bodies. Her agonizing pain was like a serpent rearing its ugly head at us, awakening us to our own dramas.

After a while, I asked her at what stage in her healing she was at. Jasareen said that she was now trying to get her life back together and was working closely with a therapist. She had gone back to night school and was taking up courses in interior design while working as a secretary and housekeeper for the Robertsons. They had created the position for her so that she could stay with them as they still had the nanny who had replaced her. She says that they are good to her and treat her more as a family member than as an employee, and the children love her.

Jasareen exclaimed regret at not having paid more serious attention to the signs of brutality that Michael had displayed towards her and for not having taken action earlier to save herself from the almost fatal attack. She does not know what is in store for her but intends to move forward, to heal and to lead a new life, like the rest of us.

We decided to take a break before we listened to Tessa's story. Miriam served us more refreshments. We had tea and some chocolate cake. We spoke about other things in an attempt to lighten the mood. I gathered from our conversation that the four of us had, in one way or another, turned to spirituality, believing in a greater force that was now guiding us and putting us back on track, on our path.

Jasareen said that she had once had a vague belief in a God while she was growing up, but when this happened to her, she became bitter and very angry with God. She had been so young and hopeful and had wanted so much out of life but instead, her world had come crushing down on her. She found herself questioning God and thought that if there was indeed a Supreme force, then he was not a very kind and sympathetic God or He would not have made her suffer like this.

It was over time, after much healing work and through interacting with her employers that she has begun to see a greater hand at work in her life. She now feels the universe speaking to her in many ways and she attributes to God, the strength she gets to carry on with life. She acknowledges her employers as a blessing from God. She said that she would not have known what to do if they had not been so ready to be there for her and to help her, physically, emotionally and financially. She is certain that God had placed them in her life for a reason.

Tessa's Story:

When it came to Tessa's turn to share her story with us, she said that even though she did not suffer verbal or physical abuse, what her husband Chris had done nevertheless impacted her a great deal and caused her much anguish. Tessa, a 32- year-old Austrian, is a university professor at one of the universities in Singapore. Her husband, also an Austrian, works at a bank. Tessa found out that her husband was having an affair when a close friend of theirs decided to spill the beans on him.

She told Tessa that she had seen Tessa's husband at a pub with this woman on several occasions, and they had seemed quite intimate. Tessa confronted her husband, but he instantly denied it, explaining to Tessa that she was just a colleague and that they were working closely on a project. They had gone for drinks after work to unwind. Tessa said that she tried hard to believe him but was plagued by a lingering unease that would not go away. She said that she even went through his drawers to see if there was any evidence of an affair but she could find nothing.

Tessa recounted how Chris had always told her that in his line of work, he would have to work late and, sometimes, would have to entertain clients. Busy with work herself and acknowledging what the corporate world was like, Tessa had initially thought nothing of his late nights, but she was now determined to find out for herself if he was really cheating on her or if his late nights were as harmless as he had claimed. Tessa said that she rented a car, went to his work place and waited for him outside his office building.

After what seemed like an eternity, she said, "I saw him leave the office with an attractive young lady. My heart sank as I followed them to a condominium. I took photographs of them entering the condominium and noted the time. I waited for a couple of hours outside the building before leaving. I was furious and hurt and at the same time overwhelmed by feelings of confusion and rejection. There were so many things going on in my mind. I kept asking myself how this had happened. I had no inkling that my husband had been cheating on me. There were no signs, well except for the late nights. Chris was always so considerate and attentive, always the perfect gentleman."

She said that they had, or so she had believed, been very much in love. They were young and adventurous and had focused on their careers. They had agreed not to have children as yet as they had wanted to put all their attention and energy into building up their careers. Their intention was to travel and to experience living and working in different countries.

Tessa waited up for her husband and when he came home that night, she confronted him. Caught with the evidence, Chris admitted that he was having an affair with his colleague and that it had been going on for six months. He explained that they had been working together on a project and had to work late, so that one thing had led to another, and he had succumbed to temptation. He promised her that he would end the affair if she would forgive him.

Chris told her, "She doesn't mean anything to me. It was just fun and sex with her. It's you, Tessa, that I want! It's you that I love, not her. I chose you to be my wife, not any one else." Tessa said, "I cried bitterly when I heard that. How could Chris betray me? I felt angry, I felt hurt, and violated. I could not say a word to him. I just sat there and cried inconsolably, my heart broken by his betrayal. After about a week of soul-searching, I suggested to Chris that we have a heart to heart talk. He agreed, somewhat reluctantly.

"We agreed that if the marriage was to continue, he had to end the affair with his girlfriend. There was to be honesty and the trust had to be restored. I suggested that we attend counselling, but he was reluctant. I told him that even though I was willing to forgive him, he had to give me time to heal and that this was never to happen again. We agreed that if there were anything that we were unhappy about, we had to address them immediately, and not sweep things under the carpet. One month later, Chris told me that his ex-lover had left the company. I was relieved.

"Frankly, I did not feel secure about him working closely with her. How could I be sure that he would not give in to temptation again, although he seemed sincere about wanting to restore the marriage. I was determined however to forgive him and give our marriage a second chance.

"Things were going fine between us. I had even managed to persuade him to attend some counselling sessions, and we were working things out between us. One and a half years after his affair, and two days before our seventh wedding anniversary, Chris dropped the bombshell. He took me out to a lovely dinner and on the way home, he suggested that we take a drive to the beach. We parked the car, walked along the beach for a while in silence, holding hands like any other loving couple, found a bench and sat down. Chris then told me in a quiet but steady voice that he had something to tell me. My heart sank instantly. I held my breath, intuitively guessing what he was going to say. I had noticed that he had been a little quiet and preoccupied at dinner but had dismissed it, thinking he was tired after a long day at work.

"Then, I heard Chris saying in a very quiet tone, 'Tessa, I want a divorce. I'm sorry. Jodie and I have a daughter. She is two weeks old. I want to marry Jodie.' I stared at him blankly. I could not for a moment comprehend what he was saying. I looked at him stupidly, letting the words wash over me before the words began to sink in. I continued to stare at him in disbelief, too stunned to say anything. I could not believe that Chris had been leading a double life while pretending to work at our marriage. I could not believe the deception and the pretence!

"My God, he had fooled me yet again, and I had fallen for it. I cried, and then yelled at him, not because I wanted him to stay—that would be impossible now—but because of the lies, because he had made a fool of me again. I was angry with myself and with him. The thought of how he must have planned his rendezvous with his lover made me cringe! I did not know this man. You would think that you would know the people you love, but looking at Chris, I realized how little I knew him. I could not forgive him. I could not forgive his deception. I could not forgive his betrayal.

"I told him I wanted him out of the house the minute we got home. I was not going to have him under my roof any longer than was necessary. I told him that I would file for a divorce. For a moment, Chris was silent. He looked at me with guilt in his eyes, and then apologised: 'I'm really sorry Tessa. This is not how I wanted it to be.'

"I responded quickly, 'Don't tell me you are sorry! Don't tell me this is not what you wanted!' I yelled furiously at him. 'All that planning, all that scheming and manipulating, and lying! I don't know who you are. You are disgusting!' I shouted at him, vehemently.

"We were quiet as we drove home, each of us, deep in thought. Chris packed his bags, and left immediately. He said he would come back for the other things. That night, I cried myself to sleep, devastated, and torn apart by his deception. I could not accept that he had not wanted a child with me but had gone ahead and had one with his lover while living with me. It was indecent. It was not something I would ever have thought Chris would be capable of. That was how little I knew about him!

"I wondered how in the first place I could have accepted Chris's denials of an affair so easily and then readily believe that he meant everything he had said about wanting me and loving me. I had been so ready to forgive him. I chastised myself, cringing at my foolishness. The pain in my heart was unbearable. I felt inadequate and undesirable. I wondered what it was that she had that lured him away from me. Where was I lacking? Where did we go wrong? Where did I go wrong? I was plagued with endless questions that I could not answer. I felt defeated. I felt abandoned. My sense of self was totally shattered," she said.

Tessa filed for divorce and has remained single for the last two years. Her contract at the university was to end in a year's time. She has been offered another posting at the University of Hong Kong. Both Chris and she had planned to work there when her contract at the university in Singapore ended. Now, she was going to Hong Kong alone. She had looked forward to having a child with him in two to three years but now that was not to be too. It has been a painful, lonely and soul-searching two years for her. She says that it will take time for her to heal, to learn to trust again.

Tessa does not know if she can ever forgive him for leaving the way he did. But she now looks forward to working in a new country, meeting new people, and having new experiences. She's glad that she has her work to keep her occupied and fulfilled, and is grateful for the many friends and colleagues who had been supportive while she was going through the divorce. Tessa spends her quiet time in nature, in meditation. She has also taken up yoga and pottery and dabbles in painting, things that she had always wanted to do but had kept putting them off for want of time. Now she says that she makes time to care for herself and to nurture and nourish her soul.

That night as I sat in my balcony with a cup of hot chocolate, listening to the rendition of ***The Elegance of Pachelbel*** playing softly in the background, I marvelled at how the universe had drawn the four of us together through our similar experiences, despite our diverse backgrounds. Who would have thought we would all meet in Singapore and share our stories?

Abuse, I guess, has no respect for boundaries: not nationality, race, socio-economic class, age or gender. Having come this far in life and having survived the trauma of my childhood and adulthood, I nurse a deep desire and hope that by sharing our stories, my book will provide a healing space for the many others who are still suffering silently, unable to speak up and empower themselves with better choices.

Tessa, Jasareen, Miriam and I had, in one way or another, tried to overcome our challenges by taking appropriate action and channelling our energies into more creative and positive outlets as a form of healing. I have taken to writing, not only as a cathartic form of therapy, but also to give voice to the voiceless, to enable women with similar experiences to come forth to share their experiences with others who may be caught in similar situations.

All four of us had to go through the process of giving voice to our emotions, acknowledging our grief, pain, bitterness and resentment. We had to surrender and accept what had transpired in our lives before healing could take place. Had we been unwilling to confront our issues and trauma and deal with the agonizing pain that surfaced ever so often during the healing process, we would not have been able to move forward.

Time, without any doubt, is a crucial element in the healing process. All of us agreed unanimously that the process entailed giving ourselves the time to grieve, to process what had happened in our lives, to go through a period of reflection and soul-searching and to acknowledge with honesty the part we ourselves had played in our life's drama. Tessa dealt with her pain by taking up painting, pottery and yoga to express herself in a creative way while Jasareen took to playing a musical instrument as a form of therapy and learned new work skills to improve herself. Miriam too had taken the opportunity to upgrade her skills, to contribute her time and expertise to others through her financial skills workshops; she also travels to new places to rejuvenate herself frequently.

It has not been an easy road for us but what has helped us to thrive despite the nightmare we have gone through is the faith and trust that we are meant for better things and that we deserve more than what we had in our past relationships: we deserve to be happy. We have come to learn, and are still learning, as part of the healing process, how to love, respect and accept ourselves, warts and all. Happiness no longer seems as elusive as it once was, only because we were willing to give ourselves another chance; we were willing to allow the healing process to unfold naturally as we moved forward on our journey to healing.

In the process, we were willing to embrace the spirit of renewal and growth: to create a space for our fragmented self and our broken spirit to be healed into wholeness. We were willing to redefine our reality by rewriting our scripts, reinventing ourselves. In other words, we were not going to give up on life. To have done so would have been to dishonour our Creator. We had more or less successfully broken the fetters that had kept us caged to our past because we had, to some extent, been successful in forgiving ourselves and our perpetrators.

Forgiveness for ourselves and for others is an important aspect of healing that cannot be stressed enough. It occurs when we are willing to see beyond the imperfections in ourselves and in the other. Without forgiveness, reconciliation of what has transpired in our lives cannot be realized since bitterness and resentment will consume us and interfere with the healing process. In order to move forward, which we have control of, we have to choose to not allow the hurt and the pain of our past determine the possibilities of our future: we have to transcend the past, no matter how long it takes or how insurmountable the challenges may appear to be, or we will end up like the people of Israel, who chose to remain slaves to Egypt instead of seeking freedom. In Genesis, we are told that when God commissioned Abraham to lead the people of Israel out of Egypt to freedom from slavery, the Israelites complained about the hardship in the wilderness. They chose instead to return to Egypt as slaves because they were provided with food and shelter. They prized material comfort over their freedom, dignity and happiness.

Victims of abuse, be it emotional, verbal or physical, often experience a great sense of worthlessness and helplessness and over time tend to lose a sense of reality of their situation. They are unable to see that they are short-changing themselves by remaining in a dysfunctional relationship. More often than not, embarrassment, poor self-esteem, lack of confidence, fear of loneliness, and fear of venturing out on their own keep them tied to their abusive partners.

Many make excuses for their partners, believing that they are themselves often to blame for their partner's angry and emotional outbursts or demands for more time and attention, or they insist that there had been times when their partner had been kind and loving, and they had enjoyed good times together. What they fail to realize is that mistreatment is definitely not acceptable. When people allow themselves to be mistreated, disregarded and devalued, they send out a message that says loudly: It's alright for you to trample on me. They set themselves up as victim and encourage the other to be the perpetrator.

In some instances, to compensate for their powerlessness, the victims assume the role of the perpetrator in an act of defiance and resistance. This inevitably serves to perpetuate the cycle of abuse as the parties involved engage in power struggles that encourage co-dependency, a state where one or both parties enable the other to act in dysfunctional ways. Inappropriate, destructive and violent behaviour is not acceptable and should, in no uncertain terms, be condoned. The four of us learned this the hard way because we had failed to place appropriate boundaries in the first place.

However, our experiences have shown that it is possible to heal, to forgive, and to empower ourselves through positive and creative means. When we allow the light or conscious aspect of our self to come forth to balance and integrate with our shadow or unconscious aspect, we claim our power to be 'who we are' in this world, for we will no longer fear to claim our space, our voice and our truth. Our experiences, though painful and unnecessary, have nonetheless made us into stronger people.

We cannot tell what the future holds for us but we have all promised to remain in contact no matter which part of the world we may end up in. I believe the universe will lead us to where we are supposed to be and what we are supposed to do. When we can sail according to the winds, that is, when we can surrender and grasp whatever life has in store for us, and take little measures, day by day, to enhance and develop the quality of our life, only then can we lead successful lives.

We are all here for a reason and have a purpose in life and each of us will have to claim and fulfil that purpose as our souls will keep nudging us to grow and to fulfil our potential to be more than we are. As Helen Keller said, "Life is an adventure or it is nothing." Our purpose in life can be an adventure if we allow it to be. It is in the journey that true happiness can be found, living moment by moment, to the fullest. As the saying goes, "Time is like a river. You cannot touch the flow of water twice."

PART II: THE RUBRICS OF ABUSE AND BETRAYAL

This section deals with the information Stacy gathered to educate herself on the dynamics of abusive relationships in the course of her healing and writing journey. It is research-based and, though brief, it offers an understanding of the psychology of abuse and the healing process.

Part II identifies:
- Characteristics of intimate relational abuse and betrayal
- Reasons why abuse takes place
- Effects of abuse
- Why the targeted do not leave their partners
- What is lacking in dysfunctional relationships

Although this book focuses on the possibilities of healing and transcending the effects of abuse as a transformational journey to selfhood, this can only occur with better awareness and understanding of the experience of abuse, ranging from knowledge of its causes to being familiar with the factors that perpetuate abuse and obstruct healing. In this section, we consider briefly, the rubrics of intimate relational abuse and violence in their varied forms.

The prevalence of domestic abuse and violence till this very day, even in societies that are deemed to be modern and progressive, makes it absolutely necessary that the general public recognize abuse for what it is: whichever form it assumes, whether physical, emotional, verbal, sexual, financial or spiritual, abuse violates human dignity and rights and damages the body, mind and soul.

Chapter 12

All violence is the result of people tricking themselves into believing that their pain derives from other people and that consequently those people deserve to be punished.

Marshall Rosenberg

What Constitutes Abuse?

Intimate relational abuse or 'domestic abuse', as it is commonly referred to, is characterized by an asymmetrical distribution of power and control between teenagers, adults or family members in an intimate relationship. There is often a pattern of intimidating, threatening or aggressive behaviour that is used by one party to control the other's actions or to cause them physical, sexual or psychological harm.

Abuse assumes its form in myriad ways: through physical, sexual, verbal, emotional or psychological, financial and even spiritual behaviours. Abuse is typically prompted by fear, hostility and anger. Often the targeted is used as a punching bag for the abuser's frustrations and inability to manage anger and hostility. It is crucial to recognize that anyone can be a victim of abuse, regardless of gender, sexuality, age, ethnicity, nationality, religion, education, employment or marital status. Even the wealthy and the highly educated can be targets of abuse.

As relationships of dominance are often immersed in patriarchal beliefs and attitudes that men have a right to dominate and control women, it is imperative that we recognize the characteristics of abuse and not dismiss certain behaviours or attitudes as culturally 'normal.' Women who have been subjected to such social and cultural conditioning have, wittingly or unwittingly, perpetuated the cycle of subjugation through their compliance.

Studies on domestic violence show that one woman in every three around the world is abused either physically, sexually or psychologically by an intimate partner, usually male. However, it is important to note that there are heterosexual and homosexual men and boys who are also targets of abuse. Although, most of these cases fall within the emotional or psychological category, there are incidences where men have sustained physical abuse that have warranted hospital emergency care.

According to international studies on violence against women conducted by the World Health Organization in 2011, 20 % of women and up to 10% of men in the world were abused as children. This is alarming as psychological studies indicate that there is a tendency for abused children, who are often products of abusive families, to either accept and submit to abuse as part of their reality or to themselves become abusers in later life, feeding into the cyclical nature of abuse.

Intimate relational abuse in any form is a violation of trust. It is one of the most devastating forms of betrayal a person can experience because it often takes place within familial and sexual relationships where one expects to feel especially safe and cared for. The betrayed person feels violated and perceives herself as less than lovable or worthy. As such, I have included the issue of infidelity as it exemplifies abuse of marital vows, commitment and trust. Infidelity is a form of emotional abuse that inflicts hurt, pain and anguish for the betrayed.

The first and most important step that you can take in reclaiming your power is, undeniably, to recognize and to acknowledge that you are in an abusive relationship, before you can even take the necessary steps to change the status quo. The gathering of knowledge is important in this stage. There are many books available that deal with the issue of abuse for those who would like to read more about it.

Some of these books that I have found particularly useful, which you may want to refer to, are listed in the bibliography of this book.

Guidelines for Recognising the Varied Forms of Abuse

Abuse is often constituted by layers of complex emotion that, more often than not, makes leaving the abusive relationship a whole lot more arduous. In such relationships, the parties involved are emotionally and psychologically overdependent on each other to the extent that they are unable to live or function without the other, which gives rise to unhealthy co-dependent tendencies. What I have listed below are but guidelines for identifying the varied forms of abuse. Some characteristics of abuse are blatantly evident as in physical abuse or sexual abuse. Other forms of abuse may be more subtle in their defining characteristics. In some of these cases, the question is often raised as to where we should draw the line that determines whether the perpetrator's act or behaviour is abusive.

In some cultures, yelling or talking in a loud, expressive and gesticulating manner is a normal mode of communication. In another culture, it is unacceptable and is deemed abusive. You will have to discern where you will draw the line in your relationships in these borderline cases. I would like to reiterate however that it is important that you be aware of definitions of abusive behaviour and not get caught up in its cycle.

Physical Abuse

Physical abuse or violence involves aggressive behaviour that results in pain, physical hurt or injury that may or may not leave physical marks. A person who resorts to physical and verbal abuse is considered a bully. The purpose of abuse is to intimidate and to show the targeted person who is in charge.

Physical abuse comprises any of these:
- throwing things at you
- using a weapon to deliberately hurt you

- throwing chemical on face/body parts
- burning with cigarettes/hot iron
- manhandling
- kicking
- bruising
- slapping
- hitting
- punching
- pushing
- grabbing
- pulling the hair
- choking
- strangling
- suffocating
- scratching
- pinching
- scalding
- cutting
- blinding
- causing death

Both Miriam and I had experienced physical abuse that took the form of shoving and slapping, which left minor bruises on our bodies. In Jasareen's case, however, the severity and brutality of the physical abuse she encountered in her marriage proved to be near fatal. It left her broken in body and spirit and deeply scarred, emotionally.

The safest thing to do in a situation that poses danger for the targeted person and her children is to remove themselves from the dangerous situation and seek help from the relevant authorities such as the police, women's shelters and women's organizations. Getting a Restraining Order may also help to ally further physical attacks, giving the targeted person time to plan a course of action.

Sexual Abuse

Sexual abuse encapsulates the notion of the man as the hunter and the woman as his game. This idea highlights the predatory instincts of the perpetrator in seeking out his prey and submitting his target to subjugation. The issue is often compounded by the utilization of mind games that further generates the cyclical effect of the abuse. The reverse however can be true too, where the woman uses the man as a sexual target to satisfy her insatiable or excessive sexual needs as a means of psychological control.

Sexual abuse involves the issues of power, pursuit, conquest and control. There is a strong undercurrent of hostility at play. It can lead to physical abuse and emotional damage. It demeans the spirit and soul of the individual as the targeted is reduced to being a sexual object and deprived of respect and dignity. Often love and respect are missing in these relationships.

Sexual abuse can be explained in these ways:
1. the forcing of unwanted sexual activity by one person on another, as by the use of threat or coercion
2. sexual activity that is deemed improper or harmful, as between an adult and a minor or with a person of diminished mental capacity
3. any range of inappropriate behaviour that causes distress or harm to an individual
4. using the targeted as a 'sexual object' to satisfy sexual desires and to assert power and control

Sexual abuse includes any of these:
- rape: non-consensual sex even within the parameters of marriage
- sexual assault
- non-consensual sodomy
- being forced or coerced into performing degrading sexual acts

- forced to watch pornography
- forced to watch sexual acts
- non-consensual orgies
- using sexual or derogatory names on the partner
- being forced to be photographed or filmed during sex
- coerced to have sex with a person other than the primary partner
- forced to be watched having sex

Miriam had to suffer the indignities of being raped by her lustful husband and forced into sexual acts that she deemed indecent and degrading. Rape, even within a marriage, is considered illegal in many countries as it denotes lack of respect and consideration for the targeted person.

Financial Abuse

Economic domination can be just as devastating for women. Financial abuse involves forcing victims to be financially dependent on the abuser by denying access and control of one's financial resources and financial information like bank statements. In some cases, independent single women who once were in control of their own income have found themselves suddenly having to hand over their pay check to their husbands and given fixed allowances upon getting married. Some have had to ask for money for their personal use and have had to account for every cent spent. Others are denied knowledge of what their husbands do with their pay check.

These women either submit to their husband's control of their finances out of fear or through compliance, as social and cultural conditioning would have them do. Inciting fear and treating women as children incapable of handling their own finances deprives them of their independence and self-respect, and is a violation of their rights.

Financial abuse takes place when the perpetrator does any of these:

- controls the purse strings/household money
- places everything from house to cars to bank accounts to check books in his name
- treats the wife merely as a buyer for the household as he considers any money given by the husband to his wife is his
- withholds money
- limits access to money
- controls pay checks
- controls personal purchases
- expects detailed account of household and personal expenditure
- denies access to any other matrimonial coffers or bank accounts other than what is given as household allowance
- refuses to provide money for medical treatment or financial support of the partner (reference is especially to homemakers)
- steals money from partner's wallet or bank account
- does not allow partner to make financial decisions or include her in such decision-making
- prevents partner from taking or keeping a job
- assumes control of partner's assets and financial resources
- makes use of partner's funds, resources, property without her consent or authorization
- expects partner to be financially responsible for the home and family while the perpetrator spends money indiscriminately and is financially irresponsible or refuses to seek employment

Religious Abuse

Religious abuse in a marriage or partnership can occur in many ways. Religious scriptures can be used by the abuser to enforce the wife's subjugation by citing the tenet that the duty of a wife is to submit to her husband. In such scriptures, the husbands are often considered to be heads of the household. Such beliefs can be abused to the advantage of the offending spouse. Religious beliefs often go hand in hand with social and cultural conditioning that supports patriarchal culture's upholding of male privilege and domination.

> Religious abuse occurs when the perpetrator does any of these:
> - forces the partner to comply with his own religious beliefs
> - creates guilt and fear if religious beliefs are not adhered to
> - shows disrespect for the partner's spiritual beliefs and values where these differ from those of the abuser
> - uses religion to dominate the partner

Emotional/ Psychological Abuse

Abuse does not always entail physical violence. Emotional abuse, which includes verbal abuse, is a kind of battering that does not leave physical evidence but may nevertheless have lasting emotional and psychological scars. It can be just as damaging as physical abuse. All forms of abuse, in fact, include emotional abuse, where emotional and psychological pain is effected through denigration and through denial of respect, love, consideration and attention to the targeted person.

The purpose of abuse is not only to undermine and devalue the targeted individual but to gain control over the person. The damage done to the human spirit is dehumanizing as it cuts through the very core of the self and leaves the targeted individual feeling confused, trapped, worthless and demeaned.

> Emotional abuse includes these:
> - any form of intimidating behaviour such as threatening to hit you, causing terror, or using the body to block the partner
> - black mailing: threats to take away the children
> - threatening to cut off financial support
> - threatening to commit suicide
> - depriving the partner of social contact with friends and family, or forbidding her participation in social or leisure activities

- denial of privacy: listening to the partner's telephone conversations, going through the partner's mail, drawers, personal items, cell phone, and text messages
- denying sleep
- manipulation through guilt
- mind games: playing 'break up' and 'make up' games
- controlling how you dress, how you eat, what you do, where you go and how you spend your money
- excessive jealousy/possessiveness: checking up on you constantly by calling you on the cell phone or text messaging you, and expecting you to respond immediately
- bullying: aggressive behaviour, treats you like a doormat, talks down at you
- teasing
- hostile jokes
- passing disparaging remarks
- treating the partner as his emotional 'punching bag', to vent his frustrations in other areas of his life
- physical and emotional infidelity
- emotional and physical abandonment, neglect or unavailability
- silent treatment or stonewalling: refusing to communicate or address your concerns, ignoring your presence
- making all the decisions for you and the family
- treating you like a servant, child, or possession

Verbal Abuse

Verbal abuse, an extension of emotional abuse, is an act of hostility. It constitutes any or all of these:
- verbal threats to kill/hurt you, your children or other family members: "I will kill you"; "You will never get away from me"; "I will hunt you down"
- using threats to keep partner from leaving or forcing them to drop charges

- belittling/insulting behaviour: teasing, poking fun at you, making you feel stupid, useless and incompetent
- making hostile jokes
- passing disparaging remarks about you, your family and friends
- name-calling: calling you 'stupid', 'Dumbo', 'hopeless', 'useless', 'good for nothing', 'fat ass', 'ugly', or 'retard'
- using derogatory names and sexually explicit language on you such as 'bitch' or 'whore'
- criticizing you or your work and capabilities
- ridiculing
- yelling
- blaming
- attacking your character
- humiliating or embarrassing you in private or public to reduce your self-worth
- trivializing and passing condescending remarks about your goals, interests, pursuits, accomplishments and beliefs
- constantly interrupting you in mid-sentence and finishing off your sentences, creating doubts about your intelligence or ability to communicate well. This reinforces the patriarchal cultural belief that men are allowed to speak to women in that manner. It denotes a lack of respect for the other as it invalidates the person.
- denial: denying the abuse or playing down its seriousness, making the partner appear petty
- shifts responsibility for the abuse onto the targeted and blames the targeted for his anger/abusive behaviour
- blames past abusive partner/s, bad childhood, or a bad day for his abusive behaviour

Steven's references to me as a 'baby elephant,' his calling me a 'nothing,' trivializing my success at work, poking fun at my spiritual beliefs, yelling and humiliating me in front of his business associates by drawing attention to the food I had prepared for a dinner party as being cold, are all instances that indicate exertion of control, lack of respect, and disregard for me: his words diminished, invalidated and dishonoured my personhood. Similarly, Miriam's husband's reference to her as a 'whore' and a 'kept woman' and his treatment of her as a sexual object that existed to satisfy his lustful demands demeaned and undermined her value as a person.

Infidelity

Infidelity entails a breach of good faith and trust. Fidelity is derived from the Latin word for 'faithfulness' (*Oxford Dictionary*) and is based on the principle of 'not deceiving another.' In the context of intimate committed relationships, as in a marriage or partnership, infidelity violates the boundaries of the relationship. It is shrouded in secrecy and involves deception and lies. It includes both sexual and non-sexual behaviour that compromises the primary relationship as time, energy, attention and priority are given to the third party and not to the primary partner or children.

Many women have dismissed or minimised their partner's emotional affairs as 'nothing,' as being 'not a big deal' out of fear of making a mountain out of a molehill or pushing the partner into the arms of the third party. Some are simply unaware that such relationships, even if these do not include sexual behaviour, are destructive to the primary relationship. They ignore the signs but subconsciously feel the discomfort and the loneliness of being displaced in their partner's lives. Infidelity destroys marriages and primary relationships as it crosses the boundaries of love and trust and is a betrayal of the commitment that the parties involved had pledged to one another. Like all the other forms of abuse, infidelity causes emotional/psychological damage to the spirit.

Infidelity often involves the following:
- acts of sexual unfaithfulness
- acts of disloyalty
- violation of the marriage covenant through adultery

- breach of trust
- deceitfulness
- duplicity
- cheating
- betrayal

Infidelity includes:

Physical adultery

Adultery is defined as "voluntary sexual intercourse between a married person and a partner other than his lawful spouse" (*Oxford Dictionary*). The notion of adultery has been expanded to include any form of "intimate extra-marital acts." Adultery is abuse of marital commitment where the promise to be faithful is a contract between the two committed parties.

Adultery denotes abuse of trust, cheating and unfaithfulness. Knowledge of infidelity, whether physical or emotional, is important in today's context as people are not only working longer hours and are in closer contact with the opposite sex, they are also travelling together on business trips, thereby increasing the likelihood of infidelity occurring within the space of a working relationship. It does, of course, happen in other contexts. Like any other form of abuse, adultery is a choice.

Emotional infidelity

Emotional affairs include non-sexual behaviour, such as flirting with one person over an extended period of time and having an intense and intimate emotional attachment or bonding to a partner other than to your spouse or the partner in your primary relationship. There is always an element of attraction and excitement involved in such relationships.

Characteristics of Emotional Infidelity

Emotional infidelity can be considered as adultery even though society has yet to recognize it as such. The same dynamic that appears in any sexual affair is present in an emotional affair. It crosses and violates marital boundaries. Emotional infidelity takes place when a partner shares greater emotional intimacy with someone other than his/her spouse or committed partner. It occurs through intense feelings, thoughts and fantasies rather than through physical contact.

There may, however, be sexual tension or chemistry and secrecy involved in the relationship. This can create excitement for the involved parties. The people around them are more often than not able to pick up the vibes. As the relationship deepens, the cheating partner may spend more time emotionally connecting and bonding with the 'special friend' and depriving his spouse of the same kind of attention, consideration, loyalty, time, energy and level of intimacy that the 'friend' is receiving.

The spouse may be excluded from social and official functions that include the 'special friend.' The involved parties start sharing intimate details of their lives with each other. The danger occurs when the cheating partner compares his spouse unfavourably with the 'friend' and starts to idealize her, projecting what he desires onto the person. The friendship may move beyond the platonic level to include flirting and seduction. As it progresses, the relationship develops in intensity, thereby heightening the excitement of the parties involved.

The intensity of the emotional affair drains emotional energy from the marital relationship. The cheating partner short-changes his spouse when he pays more emotional and physical attention to the special friend as he fails to honour his moral obligation to his partner. Emotional infidelity signifies unfaithfulness and therefore bears the same consequences of physical adultery. Emotional affairs can and often do lead to sexual affairs. In fact, emotional infidelity can be more serious and dangerous than sexual infidelity since there is deep emotional attachment to the third party.

Like me, Miriam, Jasareen and Tessa had spouses who had betrayed them physically and emotionally. Tessa's marriage had failed because of her husband's sexual and deep emotional attachment to his lover. He could not keep away from his lover despite promising Tessa that he would end his affair. His affair resulted in a child born out of wedlock with his lover. Tessa was bereft by his deception and the double life he had led while pretending to work on their marriage. She was angry with herself for having trusted him. She said that, "He had seemed so sincere. The marriage had been important to me and I had been willing to forgive his one-time indiscretion."

As in Tessa's case, many of these affairs occur at the work place as people tend to work closely and for longer hours these days, thus spending much of their awake time with their colleagues and friends or in social contexts that require frequent entertainment or travelling as part of their job scope. It is therefore necessary for boundaries to be set up and maintained if marriages are to survive today.

Partners involved in affairs, whether physical or emotional, should consider the effects on the marriage or partnership, the spouse and children as it can often lead to neglect and emotional unavailability. Partners like Steven and Chris, who chose to spend most of their hours at work and with their friends and colleagues rather than with their families, short-change their partners with their physical and emotional unavailability. Where emotional abandonment abounds, emotional divorce takes place even before the physical divorce. The emotional distance and neglect suffered in these cases often prompt the abandoned partner to question their worthiness and lovability.

Like physical infidelity, emotional infidelity indicates lack of love, respect, consideration, commitment and trust. It involves deception and betrayal. It devastates marriages and families. The cheating partners may dismiss or minimise the affair and rationalise that, since there is no physical contact, it is alright. It is not! It is important for the betrayed partner to realize that it is not alright for their partner to be spending so much time, energy and financial resources on a third party.

Infidelity damages relationships by reducing the commitment, emotional sharing and intimacy; it takes away time, attention, care, love and respect from the relationship. The energy, attention and time devoted to the affair could have been invested in the relationship, working towards solving marital difficulties and enriching the committed partnership. Boundaries of what is acceptable and unacceptable behaviour should be set and adhered to. Infidelity hurts! It causes much distress, anguish and sorrow for the betrayed partner and their children.

Abusive men, including those who commit infidelity, who are not held accountable, are given the license to continue their destructive patterns. The women who remain silent and who do not lay down boundaries are just as guilty of perpetuating the cycle of abuse. Recognizing abuse for what it is, no matter how painful the admission may be, is crucial in initiating a change of attitude and action.

Chapter 13

The limits of tyrants are prescribed by the endurance of those whom they oppress.

Frederick Douglas

The Effects of Abuse: The Disintegration of Selfhood

Acts of violation can cut to the very core of the soul, leaving the targeted subject devastated and overwhelmed. Most of us who have been targets of abuse, experience over time, a loss of selfhood, self-worth, self-respect, self-confidence and self-love. More often than not, many are besieged with a gamut of emotions that range from debilitating fear, despair, doubt, insecurity, self-loathing, guilt, anger, resentment, bitterness, sorrow, loss and grief. Many enter into depression, feel lonely, rejected, isolated, and abandoned; they feel unloved, unlovable and worthless.

Very often, the targeted are led by their abusive partners to question their sanity and emotional maturity. They are told that they are either insane, immature, over-sensitive, making a mountain out of a molehill, making things up, being 'uptight,' or being 'dramatic'; they are ignored, dismissed, discounted, disregarded, blamed for the state of the relationship or for the abuse and made to feel guilty as they are repeatedly told that it is their fault. Often perceived as insignificant and unequal in status, they are treated with lack of respect, love and consideration.

The trauma of being in an abusive relationship devalues and undermines the targeted to the point that their emotional and physical well-being is compromised when their self-esteem and perception of themselves and of life are affected. To be denigrated constantly and told that you are a 'nothing,' that you are 'hopeless,' 'frigid,' 'stupid,' 'worthless,' criticized for your appearance, skills and intelligence, and betrayed, deceived and lied to can be terrifyingly devastating.

The frequent denigration, ridicule, condescension and abuse can erode the women's aspirations, confidence and belief in themselves, their personal integrity and their personhood. Although some of these women may portray a confident exterior and may be highly competent at their work and home arenas, most of them become less confident about themselves in their personal lives as they start to wonder and question what they stand for in their partner's eyes.

Under such emotions, it takes a woman with a lot of courage, strength and determination to remain in the marriage for whatever reason, let alone make the decision to leave the relationship. Most of us are filled with guilt, shame and isolation in the fear to give voice to our plight and seek outside help. For women like Jasareen, it often takes an almost fatal attack to make them end the relationship. Women who suffer severe physical abuse should seek help from the police or any relevant authorities and shelters to ensure their safety.

There is much information available these days that will help you to recognize the signs of abuse and strategies that you can employ to help you to lay down boundaries of what you will or will not accept. Attending counselling sessions with your spouse is a good idea and can be successful if both parties are willing and sincerely committed to working at the marriage. If, however, your spouse is unwilling to attend counselling sessions, it will still be beneficial for you to attend the sessions on your own as these will build up your awareness of your situation and help you to make the right decision. The other options are to seek help from women's organizations that may provide free legal aid and counselling, or from shelters, support groups, family and friends. Whatever decision you make must come from a space of power, no matter what that choice is. It is the ability to exercise the choice that is right for you and to fully accept the consequences of the decision that empowers you.

Why Abused Women Do Not Leave Their Marriage/Relationship

The dynamics of a marriage are complex and nobody should be made to feel inadequate for not leaving an abusive relationship. This section looks briefly at some of the common reasons why women do not leave their abusive partner.

Cultural/Social Conditioning

Up to this very day, there are men and women in many societies that buy into their respective stereotypical dominant and submissive gender roles that have been ingrained in them since young. The men believe that they have to assume a masculine, macho role and assert their superiority and power over women while the women try to comply with the 'good wife and mother' stereotype expected of them by society and assume a more submissive role. It is the adherence to stereotypical cultural, social and religious attitudes that form the zeitgeist of violence as the men see it as their right to dominate the subordinate sex while women continue to perpetuate the cycle with their silent acceptance of the unequal status quo (*UNICEF*, 2007).

Although divorce rates have risen tremendously over the years and attitudes towards it are changing, the idea of a divorce nevertheless continues to indicate failure and it is still culturally taboo for some societies. The stigma attached to divorce often generates emotions of shame and embarrassment that make women reluctant to assume the status of a divorcee. Many who choose to hide behind these emotions of guilt and shame refuse to seek help from outside sources such as family, friends and support groups. Neither are they willing to take action to free themselves from the tyranny of abuse for fear of public opinion. They would rather cover up what is happening in the home so as to retain outward self-respect than to lose their dignity with their revelation. This is especially so for women in traditional and conservative societies and cultures who fear being discriminated and ostracized by their own society.

Another reason why abuse in most societies is usually kept behind closed doors is because many of the abusers display outwardly the characteristics of the 'knight in shining armour' or the 'chivalrous rescuer' archetypes. They are generous and nice with other people and are often popular and charming outside of the home. The women who do come forward to reveal that they have been abused often wind up not being believed and, worse, are dismissed for being too whiny. They thus do not receive the kind of support they need from family members and friends.

Poor Self-Esteem

Women who have suffered abuse tend to gradually lose their self-esteem and confidence. They often perceive themselves in a negative light and believe, as they have been told frequently by their abusers, that they would be unable to cope and manage alone on their own, that they would not be able to have a life better than what they have now. Instilled with this kind of fear, these women, especially the homemakers, who are financially dependent on their spouses, cling to their marriage for fear of having to cope and manage alone.

Economic Dependence

Women who leave the work-force to nurture their family, place themselves in a vulnerable position when they find themselves in an abusive relationship. The harsh reality is that when homemakers become totally dependent on their husbands for financial support and have no other financial means to support themselves, they become unwittingly, economic prisoners. Many of these men too encourage the women's dependence by not allowing them to work, by insisting that they look after the home, by controlling the finances and having all the assets placed under the husband's name, thereby depriving the women of financial means.

For the women who are homemakers as well as those from a lower income group, leaving the marriage can be a frightening prospect as they entertain legitimate fears of whether they can manage financially on their own, especially if they have young children in tow. For the better educated women who are married to men who earn high income, and who have left the workforce, leaving a comfortable lifestyle and status will inevitably compromise their standard of living.

These women however face a better chance of returning to the workforce than their lower income-earning sisters, given their higher level of education. It is crucial that homemakers and women from the lower income group educate themselves about the family law that supports and recognizes women's contribution to the matrimonial home, which thus gives them rights to matrimonial assets, to alimony and child support.

Hope, Loyalty and Love

Another reason why women stay in abusive relationships is that they nurture the hope that things will get better as time goes on, perhaps when their husbands are less stressed at work or when the children get older and they can have more time together or for other varied reasons peculiar to their marital context. Some believe that their partners will reform, others hope that they will do so, while many others hold on to love as the reason for not leaving.

They argue that their husbands really love them and are nice to them, often apologizing to them, showering them with gifts and taking them for holidays after a bout of abusive behaviour. They give excuses for their husband's actions, believing it is their duty to be loyal to their partner and protect him from public scandal. Many of these women prefer to be in denial than to face the ugly fact and see abuse for what it is.

Fear of Being Alone

Co-dependency is a psychological condition that encourages unhealthy dependency. It can manifest as addictive tendencies whereby one person is psychologically over-dependent on someone or something. The partners may believe that they can't function without each other or one or both partners may become dependent on substances like drugs and alcohol or sex, work and food. Co-dependents can also be addicted to emotions and behaviours: misery, cynicism, approval-seeking, obsessive and controlling behaviours, which emerge as habits. The underlying emotions of co-dependency are fear, insecurity and neediness. Co-dependents are generally unhappy people who look outside of themselves to fill their emptiness. Oftentimes, they seek love and attention from people who are incapable of loving them because they are unable to love themselves.

Co-dependent women who are afraid of being alone and taking responsibility for themselves, sometimes assume a child-like role in a pseudo-parental relationship: they put on masks and dance to their partner's tune in order to be accepted and loved. The dominant partner encourages the unhealthy dependency as a way to control and manipulate the dependent partner, subjecting her to his whims and fancies.

Break-Up of Family Unit

The possible break-up of the family unit is another reason why women do not leave their abusive partners. Many women adhere to strong family values and hold on to the belief that children need to grow up with both parents. They put up a brave front and try to tolerate their situation for the sake of their children. The reality however is that it is more damaging for children to grow up in a hostile and conflict-ridden home and to witness abuse than to grow up in a single family unit, where there is an abundance of love. This is especially so if they have the support of an extended family, friends and community.

Mind Games

Mind games involve manipulation and power play. In such a scenario, the dominant partner manipulates the weaker partner's vulnerabilities to elicit compliance to his demands, often making her feel guilty or anxious. Unfortunately, some of these women are oblivious of the subtle mind games that their abusive partners play on them. The abusers even go as far as to entice their partners to stay with them by faking illness, by expressing their inability to carry on with life without their partner or by threatening to commit suicide, thereby encouraging a co-dependent relationship.

Dysfunctional Relationships, a Result of Deep-Rooted Fears

Dysfunctional or co-dependent relationships, with power struggles at their core, as we have seen in the four women's relationships, are a result of deep-rooted fears and insecurities. When one partner becomes abusive, controlling and manipulative as a result of fear and insecurity residing in his shadow self, the targeted partner is placed in a weakened position. The weakened partner submits to fear and either remains passive and insubordinate, as we saw in Miriam's case, or becomes defensive, as Jasareen and myself had done.

Hostility, anger and power struggles in dysfunctional relationships create conflict, emotional and physical distance, and lack of intimacy. Pain, resentment and anger outbursts, while creating distance and separation, are in fact, paradoxically, an appeal for love, for emotional connection and bonding.

Ultimately, it is the soul that prods us to bring our shadow or unconscious self to the light and into consciousness so as to be dissolved. What is repressed in our subconscious mind must be brought to the surface for healing to take place. Until we accede to this inner voice, we will behave in unconscious ways, either lashing out at others in anger or sinking into debilitating bouts of depression or even turning to substances like alcohol and drugs, and media and material goods to alleviate our pain. When we take the time to turn inward, we gain not only insight into our own behavioural patterns, but also attain better understanding of others. Acquiring self-knowledge, self-awareness and self-love will eventually enable us to correct and transform what needs to be changed in us and in our environment for more harmonious and conscious living.

What Is Lacking in Dysfunctional Relationships?

Love and Respect

Love and respect are the foundation of a successful and healthy relationship. When a partner hits you, belittles you, abuses you or cheats on you, he has no love or respect for you. There is a lack of acceptance and appreciation of who you are. Love expresses genuine concern for the well-being of another. It is not meant to be a source of pain, humiliation and grief.

Empathy and Caring

In a healthy relationship, both members display genuine love, care and consideration for each other. They take the time to listen to each other and try to understand how and what the other person feels or is going through. There is mutual support of each other's growth and well-being.

Openness and Honesty

Honesty involves open communication of ideas, dreams and goals. Feelings, whether positive or negative, are discussed with candour. Since the partners are not afraid to reveal their vulnerabilities and feel free to be themselves, there is no need for secrecy between them.

Security and Trust

Trust is a mutual recognition between the partners of their potential goodness, honesty and integrity. Both parties trust each other and feel secure enough to talk about issues in a non-confrontational and constructive way. Competition or power struggle between the partners are minimal. If a power struggle does ensue, both parties are quick to acknowledge their part in it and deal with it, often with humour, before it creates a chasm between them.

Emotional Bonding

Emotional bonding is an important element in a relationship. Emotional abandonment often abounds in relationships that lack emotional bonding. Such relationships lack deep connection or intimacy and often tend to be superficial. Intimacy involves genuine mutual loving, caring, respect and support. It arouses feelings of tenderness, empathy and deep affection. It is free of mind games, manipulation and control. Partners with strong emotional bonding constantly feed their relationship with intimacy, frequently finding new ways to express their love to keep the flame of their relationship alive.

The Process of Inquiry, Using Questions as Signposts

The process of inquiry is an important tool for attaining self-knowledge. The self-awareness we gain from this practice makes available to us more options and choices. The following are questions that I raised for myself to ascertain what I wanted from my life. These questions can act as signposts to help you to be more conscious of the choices you can make to improve your life. Bear in mind that no matter what choice you make or what action you take, this must come from a space of empowerment, which means taking responsibility for the consequences of your choices. These questions require you to go inward to do some soul-searching and self-reflecting about what you truly want in your life.

Take some quiet time for yourself, sit down with a journal and ponder deeply over each question listed below; think also of other questions that might be pertinent to your life. Write down your thoughts as you go along. Be as explicit as possible as it will help to clarify your thoughts. It is important that you be honest with yourself, especially about the state of your relationship.

EXERCISE

You may want to reflect on these questions:
- Can this relationship be saved?

- If it can be saved, list down all the reasons why you think it can be saved.
- Are both parties willing to work at restoring the relationship?
- If you answered 'yes' to the above question, what moves can both of you make to restore it?
- If you think the relationship cannot be saved, list down all the reasons for thinking thus.
- Are you wasting energy and time on a dead-end relationship?
- Are you willing to end the relationship and to move on with your life?
- Are you willing to consult a counsellor and seek legal aid that will help you to plan a course of action?
- Will you be able to support yourself and your children?
- If you are a homemaker, are you willing to return to the workforce?
- Are you knowledgeable about family law and your entitlements to spousal and child maintenance?
- What do you want from your life? This is an important question that will influence the direction you will want to take.
- What is most important to you?
- Make a list of the things, qualities and people who are important to you.
- Why are they important to you?
- If you feel, for instance, that respect is important to you, then notice the areas in your life where you do receive this and where you do not.
- What can you do to establish a culture of respect for yourself, for others, and from others?
- How and where do you need to set boundaries for a healthy relationship?
- What is it you want from your relationships: from your partner, from your family, from yourself?

These questions, if probed at sufficient depth, will not only provide you with some guidance and clarity in the direction you will want to take in your life, they will also give you a better understanding of yourself, as they did for me.

PART III: THE JOURNEY TO HEALING AND SELFHOOD

Part III integrates psychology and spirituality to illuminate the crucial elements of healing, transformation and renewal. It stresses the importance of healing and balancing the psychological and spiritual self. As such, the holistic approach incorporates healing the body, mind and soul. It explores the concept of rebirth and selfhood through the method of looking inward at one's self.

'Inner work,' as the healing process is called, requires us to connect with our soul or true Self. It is a time that we give to ourselves for inner exploration. It is within this inner space that we are able to identify and heal aspects of our shadow self and erroneous attitudes and core beliefs in order to release self-destructive and self-sabotaging behaviour. The processes of introspection and transcendence of our shadow self and distorted beliefs are required for us to attain self-awareness, self-acceptance, self-love and forgiveness.

Stacy draws on her personal experiences to illustrate the concepts and techniques introduced in this section, so as to familiarize and ease the reader into the methods introduced later in Chapter 18. To maximize the beneficial effects of the exercises, you may want to:

1. Devote a period of quiet time to your daily inner work.
2. Take the time to prepare yourself. Find a comfortable place, close your eyes and breathe deeply and slowly for a few minutes. Allow your muscles to relax.

3. Use a recorder if need be for the questions and instructions for some of the exercises.
4. Persist. Choose the exercise you feel comfortable to start with and then work through the others at your own pace. Remember that persistence pays off. Attitude is an important factor in how successful your healing journey will be. When done on a regular basis, the practice multiplies its power.
5. Keep a journal in which you can write the answers to the probing questions used in the process of inquiry, about the insights gleaned and subtle transformations that take place. Probing questions elicit powerful answers.

This section also intends to show that traversing through these essential facets of healing and growth elevates the individual to an inner space of empowerment and authenticity.

Chapter 14

Our real journey in life is interior. It is a matter of growth, deepening, and of an even greater surrender to the creative action of love and grace in our hearts.

Thomas Merton

Self-Awareness: The Key to Transformation

The first step to transformation comes with a desire for change. My journey inward began when I made the decision to deal with my shadow self, heeding the call of my soul to change what was obviously not working for me. Although spirituality has been an important aspect of my life ever since I was a young girl, I had at some point in my life been distracted from it and had allowed the light in me to be dimmed by my life experiences. Traumatized and fragmented by these, I struggled for a long time to heal before I was able to emerge from the sacred and refining fire of the 'flaming forest.'

The key to healing and transformation is, without doubt, awareness. With self-awareness comes self-knowledge, which precipitates change. The more conscious we become of what we want from life, the more consciously we stand in our truth, the better our choices will be. Conscious choices inevitably lead to conscious living.

It is important therefore to understand that change is the only constant energy that can propel us forward to a better life. Change comes from an open and willing heart that is ready to embrace new ways of thinking and doing, from a heart that is willing to turn inward to reacquaint itself with its true inner or authentic Self. The intent to change necessitates that we re-examine our limiting belief system, attitudes and social and cultural norms. This is required because we create our reality with our thoughts, emotions, attitudes and beliefs. What we believe, we become!

Studies by Carl G. Jung, a renowned Swiss psychologist, indicate that the human mind is a very powerful tool that controls our conscious and subconscious mind. It has the power to either create or destroy us according to the beliefs, thoughts and images we constantly hold in our conscious and subconscious mind. As the creators of our reality, we manifest into our reality whatever we think, believe and focus on, whether consciously or subconsciously. If we accept the beliefs and criticism that have been ingrained in us in the course of our abusive relationships or in our childhood, that we are worthless, inconsequential, stupid, fat and sloppy, not good enough or lazy, or accept feelings of being 'unloved' or 'unaccepted' as our due, then our patterns of behaviour will inevitably invite responses from others that will turn our negative perspective of ourselves into reality. Thoughts have energy and whatever habitual thoughts and images we hold of ourselves will magnify and manifest in our lives.

Recent studies are validating what Jung and many ancient teachings have been putting forth: we, as a human race, have the innate power to either create a brighter future for ourselves with our positive thoughts, feelings, beliefs and conscious choices or destroy our world with our negative, self-destructive thoughts, beliefs and emotions. In other words, we have the innate power to transform and to reconstruct what is not working in our lives by changing our negative beliefs and thought patterns and our self-sabotaging behaviours.

One crucial element in transcending self-destructive thoughts, beliefs and behaviours is to turn inward to deal with the shadow self, that which Jung calls the personal 'unconscious.' It is the part we repress in our subconscious mind: our anger, hurt, guilt, shame, fears, jealousy, anxieties and addictions. By bringing these self-destructive emotions and behaviours to the surface and by making a conscious choice to work through them, we can transmute these negative thought patterns into positive thought patterns and behaviours. The potentialities of our inner self are boundless: within the depths of our subconscious mind lie infinite wisdom, infinite power, infinite creativity and infinite abundance. By accessing this limitless potentiality within us through our conscious choices, thoughts, beliefs and actions, we have the infinite ability to transform ourselves and our environment.

In this way, we reduce suffering not only for ourselves but also for others. Jung argues that as a part of the 'collective unconscious' that is universal, we are all inadvertently interconnected. As such, what we do to ourselves or to others, the thoughts we hold of ourselves or of others, whether positive or negative, will inevitably affect us universally. It is important to understand that we are more than our physical bodies: we are in reality, pure energy or consciousness. Our thoughts emit powerful energy particles into the atmosphere around us. Thus, they carry vibrational energy that can be transmitted to others. Therefore, the positive transformation that occurs within us can also affect our circumstances and environment in a positive way.

Barbara Marx Hubbard, a social scientist and the author of **Conscious Evolution**, elaborates on this concept by stating that all of us have the capacity to evolve as co-creators of our destiny. As we tap into the innate, infinite potential that lies within each and every one of us, we are empowered to co-create with the Infinite Intelligence, Creator, God, or True Source, whichever we choose to call the Higher Power, to become the masters of our destiny. By consciously exercising choices that honour our true Self, we bring into manifestation, a conscious life for ourselves. To live a conscious life is to live a life that is congruent with the belief of who we truly are.

As we transform from one level of consciousness to another, through conscious living, we evolve naturally. The impelling, rising consciousness that is rapidly taking place on earth at this time is awakening in us, the potential to break the shackles of not only individual domination but also social and cultural domination and conditioning in the private, public and global arenas.

Women like me, who have garnered the strength and the courage to change our unequal status quo, no longer perceive ourselves as victims but as women who have transcended our experiences. I have come to believe that as co-creators of our reality, what is manifest in our exterior life is a part of our own creation. Although the road to recovery can sometimes be arduous, renewal, transformation and rebirth are possible, as I reveal in my journey to healing and selfhood.

The Journey Inward, Connecting with Our True Self

Healing our wounds is a vital process that involves a journey into the soul where our true Self resides. All of us have an outer and inner self. The outer self is our personality or ego self. It is basically concerned with structuring our relationship to the material world, in particular with offering defense mechanisms against it. The ego self is thus made up of false elements such as the self-image we present to society. Also embedded in the ego self is the scarcity mentality that frequently manifests as an intense yearning for attention from a particular person or striving for success, wealth, fame, power, body image and so on. The scarcity belief works on the notion that there is not enough to go around. It is a belief in the lack of infinite abundance. This perception leads to a sense of unhealthy competition, craving and urgency that generates a preoccupation with physical and psychological survival.

The inner or true Self, on the other hand, transcends limitations of the material world to operate from within the space of unconditional love. Connecting with our inner Self attunes us to our inner voice, the voice that empowers us into making choices that honour our true Self, which many of us tend to ignore for fear of change, fear of being pushed beyond our comfort zone and fear of unmasking the social façade we often present to the world.

It is only in going within to search our soul and reflect on our life, on what we want in life, what is important to us, and by observing our thoughts, feelings and attitudes that we can change what is not working in our lives. We obviously cannot change things if we are not aware of them. Therefore, going inward awakens in us self-awareness that is pivotal in initiating change.

Change necessitates working on our shadow self to allow that which is repressed in our subconscious mind to emerge. It involves recognizing and acknowledging the broken and fragmented parts of ourselves and allowing the inner light that emanates from our true Self to embrace and to heal these into wholeness. It means dealing with aspects of ourselves that we have unconsciously disowned or which we have found unacceptable and relegated to our subconscious mind out of fear about confronting what we perceive to be ugly.

It is therefore essential that we devote time to our inner work to heal and to transform our negative patterns of behaviour, thoughts and beliefs in order to lead happy, fulfilled and purposeful lives. If not dealt with, there will be a tendency for us to repeat the same patterns of behaviour that invite unconscious living and for our relationships to be assailed with conflict and drama. Our repressed emotions will often manifest as perpetual fatigue and apathy, a killjoy for living life fully.

We should also be aware that repressed emotions not only keep us in perpetual pain and unhappiness, they also affect our emotional and physical health by creating illnesses such as chronic depression, heart attack, cancer, asthma and degenerative diseases. Disease is a result of dissociating from our true Self. Often, we close our hearts when we are hurt and in pain, when we do not stand in our truth and integrity or when we are in fear of truly loving and living our lives fully. In the process, we deny our true Self and move away from authentic living.

In order to honour our true Self, to lead a more balanced and centred life and develop our authentic personal power, which will deepen our relationship with our self and with others, it is necessary for us to embark on a journey inward.

The process of Inner work requires that we turn inward to:

- Soul-search and reflect on our life on a regular basis.
- Observe our thoughts, attitudes, emotions, beliefs and behaviour.
- Heal and integrate all the fragmented or shadow aspects of our self.

Dealing with our shadow self leads us into the carvens of our mind so that we can confront our inner conflicts and demons and heal the emotional and psychological wounds we have sustained in the past. More often than not, the baggage that we bring to our adult relationships stem from the pain of our childhood experiences. Unless we deal with these issues, they will keep surfacing in myriad forms, tying us to our unconscious behaviour. This is one way in which our true Self provides us with the opportunity to heal our fragmented selves into wholeness.

The greater the self-knowledge we attain through our inner work, the better will be our propensity to overcome and challenge obstacles and limiting beliefs about ourselves. We will strengthen our capacity to face adversity with courage and lead a healed, integrated and empowered life. Knowledge is power.

Chapter 15

Grant me the serenity to accept the things I cannot change, the courage to change the things I can, and the wisdom to know the difference.

Reinhold Niebur

Self-Knowledge: The Path to a Conscious Life

Inner work thus leads to self-discovery, spiritual truth and transformation. It contributes to healing through the integration of the conscious and unconscious self. It is a way to reclaim our personal power and inner freedom, the freedom that strengthens our core self and helps us be true to ourselves.

    The first step I took in the course of working on my inner self was to face and accept hard truths: the distorted perceptions I held of myself, the reality of my failed marriage, the mistreatment I received at the hands of my ex-in-laws and ex-husband, and other truths that could not be helped, such as my mother's mental illness. Through the process of surrendering to what I could not change, changing what I could, and by forgiving myself and those who have hurt me, I was able to move on with my life and embrace its sacredness.

    I had lived my life alternating between deep sadness, anger and bitterness. I had struggled with unforgiveness, consumed by anger and hurt for years, unable to heal because I could not accept what had transpired in my life. I had placed a great deal of trust in Steven, so much so that his betrayal, mistreatment and emotional neglect of my children and myself left me grief-stricken. I knew that I would not be able to find peace and happiness until I surrendered wholeheartedly and did my part to forgive and heal myself first.

As I worked on my inner self, the deep-rooted causes of my problems, beliefs and attitudes were illuminated for me to process. In the course of getting in touch with my emotions, I began to understand how and what I felt and why I behaved in certain ways. It took me to a place within myself, where I had to be brutally honest before healing could take place.

In the process, I mustered the strength to surrender my pain and hurt to God, transmuting the energies of despair by attuning myself to the higher powers of love and compassion. As spiritual teachings would dictate, it is ultimately love that heals. Within the space of surrender and acceptance of what is, or what the Buddhist refer to as the 'suchness' of things, I gradually allowed grace to flow into my life. The powerful energy of acceptance and forgiveness has empowered me with an inner strength and inner freedom to understand and acknowledge that I have the power and the inner resources to change and transform my life, to create what I desire for myself.

Through my inner work, I gained a better understanding of myself and my relationship with Steven. It opened my eyes towards acknowledging and accepting the part that I had played in our failed marriage and allowed me to release complete blame on Steven. Working on myself has helped me to identify and to accept my strengths, my weaknesses, the attractive and not so attractive parts of myself. It has given me the opportunity to not only love and honour myself but also to change those aspects of myself that needed to be changed: my self-sabotaging behaviour patterns, attitudes and beliefs. Without self-acceptance, change would have been very difficult.

By knowing and understanding who we are and what we want from life and from our relationships, we can empower ourselves to exercise conscious choices. It is when we are unable to ascertain the root causes of our responses to life: the underlying sadness, shyness, fear, phobia, anger or rage that determines our behaviour or which pushes us to act in controlling, arrogant and obnoxious ways, that we we float through life unconsciously and become entrenched in internal and external conflicts in our interaction with our self and with others.

When unresolved and unhealed, the inner turmoil and wounds will manifest as warring elements within us that are often projected and reflected in our environment and relationships. At some point, the dam within us is bound to break to unleash a tsunami of destructive emotions and behaviour that will, unfortunately, cause chaos, suffering and hurt, not only for ourselves but also for the people around us.

Disconnection from our true Self creates unhappiness. It makes us feel discontented, irritable, angry, moody and hyper-critical, depressed and, sometimes, even suicidal. It is important to be aware that in our disconnected state, we can, ourselves, become abusive: when we use the people around us as punching bags to release our feelings of powerlessness, to vent our anger and frustrations when we criticize everyone and everything. People often react in unconscious ways as a result of deep-rooted fears and insecurities, of which they are often not aware at a conscious level.

A Course in Miracles defines fear as a lack of love because 'perfect love casts out fear.' Perfect love connects us with our true Self, the seat of unconditional love. Within this space, there is no fear, anger, irritation, hatred, judgment and criticism. There are only two motivating forces that we operate from, love or fear. Most of us tend to operate from fear rather than from perfect love, which demands that we love the totality of who we are. Fear, on the other hand, is a result of unmet needs and expectations. Fear is disempowering. It stifles our potential, obliterates our light and keeps us trapped in our shadow self.

Self-Love, the Root of Selfhood

In order to embrace a spirit of transformation, growth and renewal, we must be willing to love and honour ourselves, willing to challenge the obstacles in our life and willing to break the chains that keep us bound to our painful and turbulent past.

One of the most important changes that we can make for ourselves is to love and accept ourselves. This is a crucial aspect of growth that will enable us to take the necessary measures to break free from the cycle of abuse. It can, however, be an amazingly difficult task because many of us who have found ourselves in this predicament have not loved ourselves enough and have not experienced deep and fulfilling love with others. Women who lack self-love tend to lose a sense of their own self-worth and value over time.

It is imperative that we free ourselves from the self-imposed mental prison that devalues us and limits our growth towards being who we are. We forget that we can only be abused if we allow ourselves to be abused and to be treated with disrespect, if we accept the unequal status quo and make excuses for it. Eleanor Roosevelt once said, "No one can insult you without your consent." It is we who allow mistreatment of ourselves. It is we who do not lay down appropriate boundaries to teach people how to treat us well.

Through becoming aware of what constitutes abuse, by understanding why we behave and react the way we do to people and to situations, and by taking responsibility for our actions or lack of action to change our predicament, we can change what we do, change how we think about ourselves and what we are willing or unwilling to accept in our lives.

What Is Self-Love?

When my friend Rina told me that I had to love myself first, I was baffled. The concept of self-love was foreign to me. The thought of it made me feel selfish and guilty: it seemed narcissistic to me. I was, by nature, a nurturer and have, for the most part of my life, been a caregiver to my family in one way or another. But as I turned inward and began to understand the true meaning of self-love, I learned, and am still learning, to embrace it in its full glory.

Self-love**,** as I have come to understand, is not egotism as I had once believed. It is not a narcissistic or self-indulgent love, where the 'I' or the ego predominates at every moment, in a selfish way. Self-love is really about getting in touch with our true Self, the core of our essential being, where divine love resides in us. It is about honouring our inner Self. It is about allowing our inner light to shine and to generate a radiance that attracts a deep and powerful connection with other human beings. It is in the core of our being, in our soul, that we form an authentic relationship with God, with our self, and with others.

We create authentic relationships with others when we can wholeheartedly love our self. With self-love comes self-acceptance of every facet of ourselves and acceptance of others as they are. How we treat ourselves is exactly how others are going to treat us because the relationship we have with another person mirrors the relationship we have with ourselves. If we are unforgiving, critical and hard on ourselves, we will project what is within us onto others and by the universal law of attraction, we will invite the same kind of energy from others: we will repeatedly encounter people who are intolerant of our weaknesses or failures.

It is ultimately self-love and self-respect that will prompt a desire in us to change the status quo of our unequal relationship. Women who have been abused often feel alone and isolated and fear talking about their predicament for fear of judgment. But it is important for us to realize that we are not alone and that help is available if we decide to seek it. There are always alternative options, avenues and roads that we can take to empower ourselves, as Miriam, Jasareen, Tessa and I did with our lives.

The Process of Introspection, Identifying Beliefs

Introspection is the process of attaining self-awareness by examining the nature and meaning of one's emotions and beliefs. Since self-love entails that we spend time examining our belief system, the awareness that arises from this practice can provide the energy and desire we need to make the necessary changes that will transform our life.

The following are questions that I had asked myself in my healing journey. You can use these questions to ascertain how you treat yourself. This practice will help you to identify and examine the beliefs you hold of yourself and will augment the exercises in Chapter 18.

EXERCISE

- Am I self-deprecating?
- Do I frequently focus on my negative qualities, perceived or otherwise, and denigrate myself?
- Do I recognize my essential value as a person?
- Do I respect myself?
- Do I approach myself with love and compassion?
- Do I honour my feelings?
- Do I honour the choices I make?
- Am I true to myself?
- Do I often compromise my values, beliefs and feelings to accommodate others?
- Am I a people-pleaser, often going out of my way to please others?
- Do I constantly criticize and judge myself harshly for the way I look, talk, behave, eat, or dress?
- Do I beat myself up for not being perfect, for making errors or for having made inappropriate choices in the past?
- Do I constantly find fault and criticize others because I am unhappy and critical about myself?

As we grow in self-love, we learn to recognize and appreciate our value and worth as a person. We become more patient with ourselves and with others. We are able to express our needs and our individuality without fear of compromising our selfhood. We appreciate and honour ourselves without having to resort to approval-seeking or self-deprecating behaviour.

Our rising sense of self-worth will enable us to nurture ourselves emotionally, physically and spiritually, and give and receive love, support and respect. An important aspect of self-love, which many people, especially those who have been abused, are unable to recognize is the ability to receive. It is not enough that we learn to give to ourselves and to others. The spiritual law of attraction requires that we be able to receive as well, to keep the energy of love circulating. Our ability to receive stems largely from our sense of worthiness. We attract into our world, situations and people that are either positive or negative, depending on how we assess ourselves to be worthy to receive what we most desire. The root of self-worth is self-love, and self-love emanates from our true Self.

By understanding and integrating into our consciousness the concept of self-love, we can hasten the healing process that will release us from indulging in self-sabotaging and self-destructive behaviour and open us to change and new possibilities.

There are Four Aspects to Self-Love: Self-Acceptance, Self-Respect, Self-Esteem and Self-Responsibility

Self-Acceptance

The first step to self-love comes with self-acceptance. It means accepting and being happy with ourselves as we are. How many of us can truly say that we love and accept every facet of ourselves? Can you imagine then how much more difficult it must be for someone who has been, and is constantly denigrated and treated with contempt, to love, accept and believe in themselves? Nevertheless, in order to heal and to grow in self-love and acceptance and be empowered to make conscious choices, it is important that we strive to be less critical and non-judgmental towards ourselves.

Self-acceptance means that we learn to be happy with who we are, with our personality, our physical appearance and our vocation or profession, regardless of whether we are homemakers or career women. It is essential that we learn to perceive and accept ourselves as worthy.

In order to do that, we must acknowledge and accept the validity of our emotions, thoughts and desires. This means voicing our needs and grievances as well as being compassionate towards ourselves. If we feel angry or hurt for the disrespect we have been shown, it is important for us not to dismiss or suppress memories of this. In accepting ourselves completely, we must be prepared to rescind our social masks, facades, roles and pretences that most of us use to accommodate society.

Accepting ourselves also entails acknowledging our strengths and accepting our weaknesses without apology or feelings of guilt, shame or embarrassment. We attain personal freedom when we no longer fear to be ourselves, when we no longer fear what others may think of us and hence are no longer self-conscious and self-deprecating. To live a life of inner freedom is to honour our Creator and therefore to honour ourselves.

Self-Respect

With self-acceptance comes self-respect. This requires us to have a positive attitude towards our right to live with dignity and happiness. Self-respect means having a right relationship with ourselves: that we live by our truth and do not fear social pressure; nor do we live in denial or make sacrifices that will compromise our moral values and integrity.

In addition, having self-respect entails that we recognize and honour our worth as a human being. Self-respect emanates from a strong sense of self that enables us to assume responsibility for our happiness and well-being. Since self-respect is an aspect of self-love, it is that which motivate us to invest time and energy in fulfilling our needs, whether that means nurturing ourselves with a massage, going for a movie, taking a walk, starting a new hobby, or meeting up with friends: in short, it means doing whatever it takes to make us feel happy, peaceful and fulfilled.

Because self-respect generates a strong sense of security, we know who we are and what we want in life. We are not afraid to speak our mind nor have our needs fulfilled. We are able to extend love, respect and consideration to others and to treat them the way we expect to be treated.

Self-respect ensures that we are conscious of how our behaviour and words might affect others and therefore we take responsibility for our words and actions. We do not hold on to grudges because we know that we will only hurt ourselves. Since we are aware that we are not perfect ourselves, we are more willing to acknowledge and accept the imperfections in others. It is ultimately love and respect that will enable us to practice the tenets of kindness and forgiveness and move us towards extending respect and compassion to ourselves, to others, the environment and to all life force.

Self-Esteem

Self-esteem develops naturally when we love, accept and respect ourselves. Self-esteem is essential in how we view ourselves as being worthy of happiness, love and consideration. It also entails how we experience ourselves as competent in coping with the challenges of life and in how we develop and fulfill our potential. As such, it includes understanding and embracing the tenets of self-truth and self-reliance.

The level of our self-esteem affects our relationship with ourselves and with others. What perceptions and beliefs we hold of ourselves and of others will inevitably influence how we operate in any situation: whether we tolerate any form of disregard or bullying or set up healthy boundaries in an assertive manner. The choices we make in our daily lives will leverage how much we are likely to achieve in life.

Self-Responsibility

Self-responsibility is a natural progression of all the other aspects of self-love. It is an important aspect of loving ourselves as it means taking responsibility for the choices we make in our life, the achievement or failure of our desires, dreams and goals, for our behaviour, for our feelings, for prioritizing time and energy for personal happiness and growth, for the quality of our life and thus, for our own existence.

Taking responsibility for ourselves directs us away from looking towards others for our happiness and gratification, or even towards substances such as drugs and alcohol, or towards work, entertainment sources or romantic flings. It is about being able to find peace and happiness within ourselves by getting in touch with all aspects of our self.

Self-responsibility comprises nurturing our physical, emotional, mental and spiritual lives. This includes consuming good, life-giving nutritious food, not bingeing on junk fast-food or comfort food. It means not reaching out for that bucket of fried chicken wings or carton of ice-cream or chocolates or candy as comfort food and not giving excuses that we are sad, angry, hurt or bored for indulging excessively in these.

We hurt ourselves by over-eating and over-indulging in foods that are harmful to our health. This is a form of self-abuse and shows lack of self-respect and self-responsibility. Excessive weight gain erodes our already bruised and battered self-esteem. Besides watching what we eat, we need to make time for regular exercise, for de-stressing, and for pursuing inner peace and happiness.

All the four aspects of self-love that I have mentioned above are of paramount importance in our ability to be responsible for our physical, emotional and spiritual body. Self-love involves self-care. I cannot reiterate enough that the motivation to improve our lives must come from us. It is we who have to take the first step to change. Nobody else can bring us to that point. It is we who must take the responsibility for the quality of our lives and the direction in which we want it to go. It is we who must surrender our guilt, shame, self-criticism and self-loathing to God in order to heal. We must stop crucifying ourselves and instead start to love, care and nurture ourselves.

The road to healing and transformation requires courage, effort and honesty as it requires us to delve into the inner recesses of our psyche to ascertain our truths and acknowledge the reality of where we are in our life journey. It is in transcending our painful experiences that we will be able to heal and thereby restore our sense of self which will, undoubtedly, change our lives. A healed self that is aligned with one's true Self will attract peace, love, joy, creativity and abundance.

Chapter 16

It is the law that any difficulties that can come to you at any time, no matter what they are, must be exactly what you need most at the moment to enable you to take the next step forward by overcoming them. The only real misfortune, the only tragedy, comes when we suffer without learning a lesson.

Emmet Fox

Journey into the Soul: Unmasking and Embracing Our Shadow Self

One cannot truly know the magnificence of one's light until one has dealt with the darkness of one's shadow: this is the paradox of the integration process that I have had to grapple with in my journey to selfhood. Working on my shadow self has allowed me to discover and recover my true Self. The process entailed that I acquaint myself with those aspects of myself that I had unconsciously hidden in the inner recesses of my mind as a form of rejection of myself: the self that thrives on fear, anger, pain, hurts and wounds amongst the other shadow attributes that all of us carry, in some form or other, in our psyche.

In the process of my soul-searching and reflecting, I had to rip off the filters over my eyes and undo the masks that we all wear for the benefit of the world to renounce the self-deception, denial and apathy that I was clinging to. I had to identify and understand where my erroneous beliefs were coming from if they were to be healed and balanced into wholeness. I have learned that when we confront the repressed aspects of ourselves, as painful as the process may be, they become powerful tools for our transformation. I was determined to use every available tool to get to where I wanted to go in my life. I knew that it was entirely up to me to change and shape my present, to change any behavioural or attitudinal patterns or erroneous core beliefs that had sabotaged me in my adulthood.

My personal struggle to understand and embrace these fragmented aspects of myself has not been easy. It has been an on-going process in my spiritual and healing journey as I persist in my attempts to dig deeper and deeper into the murky waters surrounding my inner being, to allow divine light to flow through me and fill me with the peace of my being. In my struggle to rise above the murky water, I have often felt like the ubiquitous lotus plant, with its roots anchored in muddy water and its flower rising above to emit its radiance.

Carl Jung said, "Without pain there is no consciousness." I had not wanted to believe it when I first came across it but now I realize how true it is. Adversity is a fact of life. All of us face some form of difficulty. It is how we choose to respond to the challenges that life throws on our path that will determine the extent of our suffering. We can either choose to learn our lessons and grow from them or we can allow them to debilitate us and remain stagnant.

The pain of healing is inescapable as it often brings to the surface unresolved hurts and fears for us to confront. None of us wants to go through pain and suffering and none of us deserves to be abused or mistreated. But having gone through the abuse, I have learned that transcending these experiences and drawing lessons from them has made me not only a stronger person but also more understanding and compassionate towards those who have suffered adversities.

Thoughts have Power

One of the essential tools that I used to transcend my experience of abuse was to examine my core belief system, attitude, emotions and behaviour patterns. Self-examination is a pivotal healing practice that aids in transforming our limiting negative perceptions and beliefs. Our thoughts have the power to change our reality. As the saying goes: as he thinketh in his heart, so he is. So what we think and believe of ourselves is exactly what we become.

The mind, as Jung suggests, is a powerful tool that can be used to advantage to transform our reality. It has been described as a powerful computer that stores data that we receive from our world in our memory cells. The subconscious mind receives and accepts messages or input about ourselves from our parents, grandparents, siblings, teachers, friends, religion, media and society as truths. These become our core beliefs. Whether they are positive or negative, these beliefs become an integral part of who we think we are, the identity that we display to the world.

Unfortunately, the root causes of our pain and suffering are mostly derived from the negative emotions or beliefs that have been ingrained in us from childhood. They play an immeasurable part in influencing and shaping our perceptions, our behaviour, our actions and how we relate to others and to life in a negative way. Every time we are invalidated, demeaned, insulted or mistreated, we formulate negative images and messages about ourselves. The hurt we sustain in these instances makes us close our hearts and, over time, we become numb as we build up defence mechanisms and walls around us to keep not only people at a distance but also our emotions at bay. Others become excessively angry, defensive and suspicious of people in their attempts to protect themselves from further pain.

Paradoxically, in wanting to protect ourselves, we end up sabotaging ourselves from experiencing love and happiness through keeping people at a distance. We hurt ourselves further by replaying old tapes that keep our wounds open and bleeding, that in turn fuel and keep alive the victim energy in us. We get so caught up in this never-ending cycle of perpetual pain that we end up losing our sense of self and reality.

If our wounds and negative self-images and beliefs are left unhealed and repressed from our conscious mind, we will keep repeating the same patterns of behaviour our entire lives: we will behave in self-deprecating ways, accept rude behaviour and bullying, and keep attracting people into our lives who will reinforce our negative emotions and self-perceptions. In the course of it all, we will remain stagnant and powerless to change our reality and situation.

The people and events in our lives are the mirrors of our internal turmoil. We tend to project what is repressed in us onto others in order for healing and balance to be restored. Discordant energies that are rooted in fear, insecurity, pain and despair within us serve to create more disharmony in our relationships and environment as the universal law of attraction dictates that what is 'without' reflects what is 'within.' Our external life is but a mere reflection of what is going on in our internal life. Thus, if our external life is in disarray, we need only to look within ourselves to determine the cause.

The road to healing and to empowerment therefore begins with understanding our past, since we are the products of our belief system. In re-directing our beliefs towards greater fulfillment, it is necessary for us to exchange the negative core beliefs that limit our potential and keep us rooted in pain for positive beliefs that help us to grow and expand with love. It is imperative in the course of healing that we release conditioned habits of guilt and shame and not berate ourselves over our past choices. To indulge in such behaviour is unproductive as it ultimately boils down to self-loathing and, therefore, to self-abuse.

The power lies within us to transcend the limits of our beliefs that have kept us trapped in self-destructive behaviour and in dysfunctional relationships that are ever so damaging to our souls. It is in our power to change our distorted perceptions of ourselves and to empower ourselves by taking responsibility for our choices and actions, no matter what their consequences. By accepting, loving and embracing all aspects of ourselves honestly, by reversing old tapes and tuning out our grievances and victim stories of the past, we will ignite the desire within us to transcend our past. And in doing so, we can move forward to appreciate and embrace the sacredness of life as we invite healing, solutions and resolutions into our lives.

Understanding Our Shadow Self

In dealing with my core beliefs, I had to deal with my shadow self. As explained earlier, the shadow self is a term introduced by Jung to explain the hidden, unconscious, fragmented aspects of one's self that are repressed from one's awareness and lie hidden in the subconscious mind. Though repressed, they nevertheless impact our thoughts, behaviour and the choices we make. Each of us has shadow patterns that need to be brought into awareness and dealt with if we want to live authentic lives.

Since the human psyche is the sum of the conscious and unconscious self, it includes both the light (conscious) and the shadow (unconscious) aspects of one's self. The shadow self encompasses the rejected or unacknowledged parts of our psyche and the undeveloped potential which the ego or personality has repressed or never realized fully. It includes qualities, emotions and behaviours that do not often fit our social masks and are deemed inappropriate by society: rage, anger, resentment, fear, arrogance, greed, sadness, timidity, jealousy, manipulation, tardiness, laziness, depression and addictions.

Our shadow self remains repressed and denied because it does not want to be exposed for fear of being judged, rejected or denied love by the people around us. As a result, we wittingly or unwittingly wear social masks to fit in with societal and cultural norms: we smile when we are in fact sad or enraged; we go along with ideas that we inwardly oppose; we comply with societal norms and peer pressure and pretend to be who we are not in an attempt to be like everyone else. In the process, we lead unbalanced and inauthentic lives that dishonour our true Self.

What is unconscious in our psyche is most often projected on to others, who become the scapegoat for our repressed emotions: repressed anger, fear and inauthentic living can surface as abuse, sarcasm, hostility, bullying, addiction, deception (sometimes manifesting in extra-marital affairs), dependency, aggression, anxiety, depression and chronic fatigue. These are forms of destructive and dysfunctional behaviour that cause much inner turmoil and pain for the individual and the people around them. According to Jung, everyone has a light and dark shadow self. This reflects our human foibles. In order for us to lead emotionally healthy and purposeful lives that is in alignment with our soul, that which is repressed in our subconscious mind must be brought to consciousness to be integrated and balanced into harmony.

Why Is Shadow Work Essential to the Healing Process?

- It enables us to recognize and understand the attitudinal causes of our self-destructive and self-sabotaging emotions and behaviour.
- It helps us to understand why we keep attracting the same kind of people and relationships into our lives and why we have not learned from these experiences.
- It enables us to understand how we project what we do not like in ourselves on to others, that our hostility towards certain people may signal our own internal issues.
- It gives us a chance to correct our distorted beliefs, misperceptions, emotional reactions and behaviour.
- It helps us to heal our relationship with our self and with others.
- It frees us from notions of victimhood.
- It allows for self-acceptance of who we genuinely are.
- It helps us to be aligned with our soul.
- It opens up our hearts and allows love, abundance, creativity and joy to flow through us.

Our shadow aspects manifest as trials and tribulations in our life, or what John Cross, the 18th century theologian, refers to as the 'dark night of the soul,' and what is personally for me, the 'flaming forest'. How we deal with these will influence the future course of our life.

Integrating and harmonizing all the fragmented aspects of our shadow self through self-reflection, self-observation and self-scrutiny is a necessary journey inward that enables us to get in touch with our true or authentic Self. Connecting with our true Self not only promotes personal and spiritual growth, it is an essential element for unlocking the latent power within us. Inner work is an on-going process that will require courage, patience, commitment, perseverance, and diligence.

Identifying Shadow Archetypes

Aspects of the shadow self often surface in our relationships as lessons for us to learn and to grow from. Jung refers to these different aspects or sub-personalities of the self in terms of specific archetypes. These are some common examples:

- The deprived child archetype throws tantrums or becomes depressed and sad when expectations and needs are not met.
- The wounded child archetype relives the past and holds on to memories of neglect, abuse and other traumas endured in childhood.
- The warrior archetype gives in to anger and will wage a war as a defensive response to a threatening situation.
- The rescuer archetype fits in well with the Romeo archetype, the type who needs to conquer and protect the timid and powerless.
- The victim archetype has issues with control and power and needs to learn how to construct personal boundaries and develop self-esteem.
- The saboteur archetype constantly sabotages efforts to be happy or successful as a result of not feeling good enough.
- The queen archetype needs to be in control of every situation. She devours power, often imposing her own will on others as a way to maintain an image of superiority and to compensate for her own state of powerlessness.

- The critical parent archetype finds faults and is critical of everyone and everything including themselves.
- The prostitute archetype will do anything to compromise the body, mind or spirit for personal gain. Those who remain in an unfulfilling and unhappy marriage or in an unsatisfying job for financial gain and security fall into this category. This archetype highlights the inability to live by one's truth.

Many of us have more than one archetype working in us. It is our awareness of the different aspects of these archetypes in us that can hasten our healing process and enable the light or positive aspect of our shadow self to work for us.

Through self-examination, I was able to identify the wounded child, the victim, the saboteur and the warrior archetypes working in me. While the shadow aspects of these archetypes had kept me tied to my negative emotions, the light aspects of the shadow self had worked positively for me. For instance, while the shadow aspect of my wounded child archetype had kept me chained to my past memories, to the pain and hurt, to anger, resentment and blame, its light aspect evoked in me empathy, compassion and forgiveness for those who had hurt me.

Similarly, while my warrior self had brought up in me my defensive armour and had impelled me onto the war path to defend myself in my marriage, it was the light aspect of it that helped me not only to survive and to protect myself in a hostile environment but also to plod on through life with fortitude.

According to Carolyn Myss, author of the **Sacred Contract**, most of us have the wounded child archetype in us and carry the energy of the wounded spirit. Somewhere along the journey of our lives, we would have been wounded one way or another by someone or by some traumatic event or encounter. These wounds that are repressed in our subconscious mind may become activated in the face of external triggers: someone may do something or say something to trigger the pain in us and cause us to react in an unconscious way.

Eckhart Tolle explicitly explains in his books *A New Earth* and *The Power of Now* that the wounded energy that is trapped in our psyche often manifests as that which he refers to as the "pain body." This pain body acts like a monster in initiating reactive and self-sabotaging behaviours. It anchors us to our unconscious behaviour until we attain sufficient self-awareness to bring it to the light for healing.

Reading *A New Earth* helped me to understand how and why I reacted to my pain body, which carried the wounded energy of childhood rejection and abandonment. I realized that often my pain body would be activated when situations occurred to trigger off my still unhealed issues. Each time it happened, my growing awareness of the deep-rooted causes of my pain enabled me to bring it to the light for healing through myriad techniques such as deep breathing, meditation, prayer, energy healing, visualization, and affirmation. I also addressed the issue with the people involved wherever possible as well as forgave those who had hurt me. Please refer to Chapter 18 for techniques.

In most cases, awareness or awakening to one's true Self arises when the suffering and pain of crises incurred in traversing the 'dark night of the soul' become so intense that it is too much to bear. Jung explains that the psyche always looks for balance and integration of the fragmented aspects; it seeks healing into wholeness. As a result, we will unconsciously attract people into our life who mirror our unresolved issues, who are drawn to us by our energy: our interaction with these people will provide us with more opportunities to heal this fragment of ourselves. If we don't learn the lesson the first time, the universal law of attraction will keep on providing us with more chances to work through our issues.

A woman who has problems with laying down healthy boundaries will keep inviting people who will cross her boundaries until she is able to learn her lesson and heal that aspect of her that feels unworthy, allowing her finally to take appropriate action to establish meaningful boundaries. An addict will attract an enabler while a victim will attract a perpetrator in order for them to learn their lessons and to heal their issues of unworthiness. It is only introspection on how we are operating in our life that will enable us to choose an alternative behaviour.

Unless we consciously seek to accept, heal and grow from these shadow aspects of ourselves, the lessons will continue to emerge in our relationships as dramas, conflicts and power struggles. The warring elements within us will create unhappiness and keep us emotionally unbalanced until we heed the call of our soul to heal our inner turmoil and return to equilibrium.

Attaining awareness of our archetypes, our motivations and agenda can be useful in identifying our patterns of behaviour and thinking, and in understanding why we have attracted abuse into our lives. We do ourselves a disservice if we do nothing to heal our wounds because we may carry these wounds as our baggage for the rest of our lives, keeping us trapped not only in pain, anger and distrust but also tied to our painful past and to an unconscious way of living. Our unhealed wounds and shadow patterns become our shackles and obstruct us from our infinite potentiality, dreams and happiness. The negative energies that disconnect us from our true Self block grace, joy, creativity and abundance from manifesting in our lives.

To bring our fragmented selves into wholeness is therefore to allow our darker (unconscious) aspects to be embraced and to be integrated with our light (conscious) self. Healing demands that the wounded and traumatized inner child in us be returned to its natural state of infinite joy, peace and love.

Chapter 17

To the extent you hide your feelings you are alienated from yourself and others. And your loneliness is proportional.

Dorothy Corkille Briggs

Self-Reflection: Identifying Core Emotions and Beliefs

Although I did not seek professional therapy and instead chose to work on myself, I would strongly recommend that seeking help from a trained therapist to heal and understand your shadow. The techniques that I used in my journey to healing, which I share with you in this book, can however augment the professional help you might wish to seek.

Besides identifying my shadow archetypes and beliefs, one of the several steps that I took to heal my shadow self was to learn how to identify the emotions that surfaced when I revisited certain scenarios in my past through visualization and recapitulation techniques to ask myself what I could learn from them. Please refer to Chapter 18 for the method. In the course of reflecting on them, I had to raise several pertinent questions. You may want to do the same for yourself when you engage in the process of self-reflection. There are more questions to work on in Chapter 18. This is an important part of the healing process and should not be overlooked as it provides better understanding of the self, which is required for you to exercise choices that are right for you.

EXERCISE

These are examples of the questions I asked myself during self-reflection:

- What am I feeling?
- Why am I experiencing separation anxiety?
- Where is this deep anger coming from?
- Who am I angry with?
- Why do I feel rejected and unloved?
- From which part of my life does the issue of abandonment arise?
- Why did I attract someone like Steven into my life?
- Which aspect of Steven was I mirroring and vice versa?
- What am I supposed to learn from my emotions?
- What are my patterns of behaviour and attitudes?
- How do I react and respond to life?
- What do I want out of life?
- What is important to me?
- What can I do with what has transpired in my life?
- How can I turn my life around to enable me to grow from this experience?
- How can I change my negative emotion of grief to generate positive energy and creativity to enhance healing and be aligned with my Soul's purpose?
- How and what can I do to move on from here?
- How can I celebrate the sacredness of life?

Reflecting on these questions was no easy task. It brought to the surface, deep-rooted angst and anger, but I knew that it was absolutely necessary that I confront them in order for healing to take place. In the course of my healing, I learned through meditation to quieten the inane chatter of my active mind, which obsessed on my grievance story. I also began to be able to identify, relate and connect the emotions that emerged from my past to the emotions that I was experiencing in the present.

For instance, a loved one would say something or behave in a manner that may trigger deep pain in me, often more intensely felt than it needed to be because it had set off a certain emotion linked to the past such as my emotional abandonment issue, which had started from childhood. I soon grew to realize that there are always different perspectives to a situation and that we sometimes tend to react from our victim mode and become overly defensive, reactive, sullen, withdrawn, sad or depressed and blame others for our poor choices.

The process of healing does not take place overnight. Our habits and attitudes are often so ingrained and deep-rooted in us that it takes time to unearth and transform them. There is however no escaping but to go to the root causes of our emotions and erroneous beliefs. I have often felt tempted to turn tail and run away from these painful emotions. I was afraid to confront them, afraid to face my fears, to closely scrutinise that which I did not want to see and accept in my life. It is always easier to live in denial than to face the truth. But denial hurts.

As I persisted and began to understand where certain emotions were coming from, like my deep, welling anger at not being loved the way I had wanted to be loved, I allowed myself to embrace the pain ruling those emotions and released it to the universe. This was done through the process of surrendering in my moments of prayer or meditation. Where once, I had inexorably held back my tears when the pain and hurts had become unbearable and instead had become numb and withdrawn or fiercely angry, I found that, as the healing progressed, I allowed divine grace to soften my heart, to allow my tears to wash away my deep seated hurt.

I gave myself the time to grieve the loss of a long term, albeit dysfunctional relationship and the break-up of the family unit that had meant so much to me. In the course of observing my shadow self, I learned that I had the power to change what was no longer desirable or useful in my life.

Understanding My Shadow Attributes

My self-reflection unearthed the following emotions that had assailed me since childhood. I hope that this sharing of my inner work with you will encourage you to embark on your own healing journey.

Separation Anxiety

It was while I was engaged in the healing process of revisiting my childhood during meditation and visualization that it dawned upon me that many of the emotions and baggage I had carried into the present were largely influenced by my childhood experiences and perceptions. It regurgitated emotions that I was unaware of until I confronted my deep-rooted hurt and wounds. Because of my mother's emotional unavailability and inability to care for me at birth, I grappled with issues relating to separation anxiety and emotional abandonment.

The fears evoked in me as a child developed further when I experienced rejection and verbal abuse from my ex-in-laws, and then more rejection and abuse from Steven, all of which further reinforced my image of myself as unlovable. These experiences had subconsciously left me with a sense of feeling unworthy.

I learned through my studies that anxiety experienced in the present can be attributed to a past event or person that had produced pain and fear. Psychoanalysts John Bowl, Cindy Hazan and Philip Shaver agree that separation anxiety is often experienced at birth where there is a lack of maternal bonding or when the child is physically separated from the main caregiver. The trauma experienced typically manifests itself as crying and distress. The child, sensing the lack of warmth and security in its environment, becomes distressed and reacts with incessant crying.

Separation anxiety at a very early age inevitably creates fear, sadness, depression, clinging and a pervasive sense of emptiness. What emerges from these experiences is the fear of being separated from loved ones, from close relationships and human contact. This insecurity can manifest into a bigger problem in later life if not addressed, as it did in my case. Inevitably, it also creates emotional dependence and attachment problems, making one's removal from an unhealthy relationship all the more difficult, even in adulthood, as the realization of the impermanence of one's environment creates deep anxiety.

Psychologists like Michael V. Bloom also argue that when one's early life is too traumatic or intense for the individual to be emotionally present, what ensues is a sense of numbness, a shutting down of emotions or withdrawal. Sometimes, the individual slips into denial, to avoid confronting the pain of the issue. These are natural defence mechanisms that people who undergo trauma adopt to secure their survival in a hostile environment.

In my case, I had perceived my childhood to be hostile since my home environment was conflict-ridden and my main caregiver, my mother, was, in my young mind, hostile and withdrawn. I had felt displaced in my parent's affection when my brother, Patrick, was born. This had subconsciously made me feel insecure and unworthy of their love as Patrick was the son they had been coveting for a long time and whom they doted on. I attribute this anxiety experienced in my childhood to the fear of leaving Steven, whom I had held in high esteem, having placed him on a pedestal in the early years of our marriage. When the love that I had expected from Steven had not been forthcoming, I suffered tremendously, experiencing once again the bleeding wounds of rejection I had experienced from my mother.

Although I was unhappy, I remained in the marriage because the idea of an intact family unit, despite its dysfunction, had provided me with a sense of security and stability that I had yearned for, having come from a home that lacked emotional stability. And so, paradoxically, I believe I clung on to the marriage despite the fact that it was as unstable as my childhood.

Emotional Abandonment

My issue of emotional abandonment arose as a result of my mother's emotional unavailability, which I had unfortunately perceived as a form of rejection and as a sign of being unworthy of her love and attention.

It was through my inner work that I was able to make the connection of how feelings of abandonment and anger that had stemmed from my mother's lack of interest in me played out in my adulthood, magnified and fuelled by Steven's emotional neglect and indifference.

My anxieties about abandonment were further heightened by the fact that I had never really had a childhood: that I had been compelled to practically grow up overnight to assume my mother's role in caring for my younger siblings whenever she was too ill to care for them. My children too had suggested to me that I had probably also experienced a sense of abandonment when my father, who had been quite ill at one point, left me to take care of my younger siblings so that he could recuperate at his sister's home. I may also have felt abandoned by my three older sisters, two of whom had already married by then.

Indifference, lack of validation and emotional neglect often sear the soul and leave lasting emotional scars. Studies show that the loss of a significant figure in one's life, whether physically or emotionally, can not only intensify the longing for the attached figure and the desire for connection, it can also be accompanied by anger and anguish. The neglected person will strive to gain the attention of the significant figure in any way she can because, to her, any attention is better than no attention.

Human beings have an innate need to be touched, nurtured, recognized and validated by people, especially loved ones. It is the soul that desires deep emotional connection and intimacy. The lack of positive stroking or emotional intimacy often has detrimental effects on people, especially children. It creates an abiding sense of emptiness and loneliness, and a craving for the void to be filled.

Given my difficult childhood and marital life, I arrived at the conclusion that I was not loved and accepted for myself. No matter how much I had tried to do my best in my endeavours as a child, it seemed to me that my efforts were never good enough as my father was seldom forthcoming with praise, except to say: "You can do better than this." In the same light, Steven's criticism of my efforts and achievements left me feeling unaccepted for who I was. His name-calling and belittling had eroded my self-esteem to such an extent that it affected my perception of myself. For the most part of my married life with Steven, I felt discounted and disregarded. This made me feel very angry and I reacted defensively.

I had to grapple with my issues and to see them for what they were. I had to wrestle with my anger, resentment, bitterness and grief for a long time. The deeper I dug into the sludge, the more intense and painful were the emotions that surfaced. I knew that no healing, let alone forgiveness for myself, for Steven and for others could occur until I was ready to accept these emotions and to change the perception of myself and of my situation.

In the process of self-discovery, it dawned upon me that although one part of me had felt unworthy and unloved and was afraid and shy, which I attribute to my victim and wounded child archetypes, there was another aspect of me that was resiliently strong and determined. I was strong in what I believed and held true to my beliefs, which inevitably became a source of conflict between Steven and me. It was the warrior self in me that had given me the strength to bulldoze my way through the rejections, dejection, fears and despair to pursue my graduate education, to work as an educator, move into volunteer work, pursue my spiritual life, run my home and care for my children and parents.

At the same time, it was also this warrior self that had set me on the war path and prepared me for the attacks and criticism that I felt was coming my way from Steven. Through the healing process, I became aware that, although I pursued aggressive tactics as a defence mechanism to protect my selfhood, by resorting to such methods, I had unwittingly, to some extent, perpetuated the cycle of abuse.

Defensiveness as an Aggressive Tactic

Not having the skills to deal effectively with Steven, I resorted to defensiveness as a way to assert myself with him. I had learned over the years how to fight fire with fire. I was terrified of him dominating me into total submission. I felt suffocated by his arrogance and his controlling and domineering ways. I feared losing myself in this relationship, of being totally engulfed by an all-consuming fear of annihilation. So I resorted to asserting my identity in the only way I knew.

Psychologists argue that the danger in employing defensive tactics to assert ourselves in our relationships is that in order to maintain control and to retain a sense of selfhood, the targeted person may sometimes resort to the same aggressive tactics as those employed by the perpetrator. The experts believe that aggression as a defence mechanism involves control elements and is often about power struggles and not about self-assertion. The underlying emotion of aggression is fear, which activates the 'fight or flight' mechanism. In the case of aggression, it activates the 'fight' impulse, impelling the targeted to take action to regain control.

Aggression, in any form, whether by the perpetrator or as a defence mechanism by the victim, invades a person's personal space and boundary. In resorting to the same tactics, the victim ends up playing into the power game and does the same thing as the perpetrator. The ensuing battle for power carries on between the parties with neither actually winning the game.

The perpetual conflicts and quarrels characteristic of dysfunctional relationships serve to worsen the situation for all the people involved, especially for the children caught in the crossfire between the parents. Often it is the children who suffer great emotional and psychological stress, which can manifest as physical illnesses or in emotional or psychological behavioural problems. The reality is that there is more pain, suffering, hardship and brokenness for everyone involved. And the saddest thing of all is that, very often, the same cycle of relating may be perpetuated by the next generation, by the children who may not know any other way of relating other than what they had observed in their family environment.

Fear of Intimacy

As Robert Burney, author of *Co-dependence: Dance with Wounded Souls*, says, at the root of all co-dependent and dysfunctional relationships lies fear of intimacy, which is ultimately the fear of being hurt and controlled. Dysfunctional relationships stem from the fear of emotional abandonment, betrayal and rejection and are most often experienced in early childhood. They are more often than not perpetrated by parents, who were most likely to have been emotionally abandoned and wounded themselves. The paradox of human experience is that while human beings thrive on human contact, intimacy and close relationships, which require human connectivity and emotional bonding, fear of intimacy abounds when people undergo traumatic experiences. Most of us who have not worked on our shadow self will ultimately find ourselves in some form of dysfunctional relationship with our self and with others.

Psychologist R. D. Laing explains that some people who experience fear of commitment or intimacy, which gives rise to irrational feelings of entrapment and suffocation or of being controlled by their partners, will find any excuse to leave the relationship. They may not leave the marriage physically but may do so emotionally, mentally and spiritually, leaving their partner feeling unhappy and unfulfilled in the marriage without emotional bonding and connection. They unconsciously erect barriers and walls around themselves to safeguard themselves from getting hurt.

In this way, they close their hearts and shut themselves off emotionally from experiencing intimacy. Very often it is the partner who thinks he/she did not want to end the relationship that is the one who leaves it first, often emotionally. In such cases, emotional divorce may take place for some time before legal divorce is initiated. Some others, who believe that their partner would not want to stay with them because they are unlovable, will find ways to sabotage their relationship and will inadvertently push their partner away, thereby manifesting the very reality they feared with their partner actually leaving them. This will worsen their already low self-esteem as they now have the rejection as proof of their being unworthy of having a loving relationship.

Fear of intimacy promotes separation and division from oneself and from others. The alienation or lack that we feel within ourselves and the separation we feel from others keep us rooted in our unhappiness. This generates difficulties in relating and interacting on an authentic basis. Very often, it is the fear of intimacy that prompts us to behave in superficial, rigid and controlling ways, in an attempt to maintain some form of control over our lives and from getting too close to another person. To add to this, the lack of self-awareness that manifests as a refusal to acknowledge one's own share in the failure to bond and in having created one's own suffering sets the trajectory for the blame game and the victim-perpetrator cycle of abuse.

Psychological Denial

The moment I was forced to confront and acknowledge Steven's mistreatment of me, the denials and excuses that I had so carefully constructed to protect my selfhood, even as I was battling waves of unhappiness and depression, came crushing down. I could no longer hide in my tower of make-believe. Denial, a co-dependent characteristic according to psychologists, is an unconscious defence mechanism that is characterised by a refusal to acknowledge painful realities, thoughts and feelings.

For women who are especially economically dependent on their spouses, who fear being alone and taking responsibility for themselves and for their children, denial seem to be the easiest way to cope with a painful situation. Women who dismiss or trivialize what the offender has done by making excuses for him are minimizing the legitimate damage done to them. In the short term, psychological denial can help a person to maintain her sense of self and her sanity, which could otherwise be threatened by the acknowledgement of a painful truth or reality. Denial can help the person to function on a daily basis.

Psychological denial however leads to self-deception. It results in alienation and estrangement from oneself and from others. Since it takes tremendous effort and energy to maintain a veneer of denial and assume a facade or mask to pretend to the world and to ourselves that everything is 'perfect', the denier is often left in a state of apathy and passivity. Many women who strive to live up to social expectations, who thrive on social propriety and appearances, are devastated when they are confronted with the reality of their situation. Denial can cause great harm physically and emotionally to the denier and those around her. Often, there is a deep fear in dealing with the pain and in looking inward to see what we do not want to accept in ourselves and in our loved ones: the shadow self that all of us have within us that needs to be reconciled with and integrated into wholeness in order for us to lead an authentic life.

Anger

For a long time, I held on to anger and resentment within me that would spew out as rage. I was disappointed that my personal life was not unfolding the way I had wanted. I had all these expectations from life and from my loved ones. I could do nothing but watch all of them go awry even as I tried desperately to cling on to them. Through my mindfulness meditation practice, I learned that it is this clinging on to expectations and desires that create suffering. The anger I was holding on to in my body caused me tremendous pain, physically and emotionally.

Anger stems from fear. As R. D. Laing explains, anger can be accentuated when there is an impending fear of annihilation of the self and a fear of persecution. These emotions serve to create a distancing from one's true Self, which eventually leads to a sense of deep loss, of something vital missing in one's life, a vacuum that desires to be filled. Such was my relationship with myself, my mother and with Steven until I turned to the source of my being and connected with my true Self. Studies have shown that in the long term, repressed rage, when not dealt with in a healthy way, can manifest as deep sadness, depression, fatigue, hostility, frustration. Negative emotions and imbalances wreak havoc on individuals and the people around them.

Repressed emotions may also manifest as physical illnesses since the mind, the heart and the nervous system are all connected. The damage that repressed emotions can inflict on mental, emotional and physical health can be devastating. Being constantly angry and defensive cost me my health. My asthma was an indication of how suffocated and overwhelmed I had felt in my marriage to Steven. Both my children were also badly affected physically and emotionally as they grappled to make sense of their reality in an unhappy and emotionally destructive home environment. Thus, dealing with our repressed emotions is an important part of the healing process that should not be overlooked.

Caregiver Role

My initiation into the caregiver/nurturer role began when I was about 13. Nurturers tend to be 'mother figures.' They care, support and nurture their loved ones. The problem arises when nurturers have difficulty placing boundaries because of their inability to say 'no' to others. They tend to overcompensate by trying to take care of everyone else's needs but their own. They become over-involved and entangled with the emotions and problems of others. They will go an extra mile and try to fix things or solve other people's problems. They are often taken for granted and pushed to their limits because they see it as their responsibility and duty to look after everyone. Such care-givers are co-dependents as they encourage unhealthy dependency.

Sometimes, care-givers over-extend themselves to the detriment of their health. Then it becomes self-abuse as it indicates a lack of self-love and self-care. Nurturers like me have to learn how to take better care of ourselves, to take time out to nurture and nourish ourselves physically, emotionally and spiritually and to learn how to place boundaries when we are over-extended by demands from family, work and other responsibilities. My healing process has enabled me to be aware of my interactive behaviour, attitudes and beliefs and has created the opportunity for me to change and to grow in a healthy way.

Co-Dependency, the Heart of Inauthentic Relationships

Co-dependency is the root of all inauthentic relationships. Most of us have tendencies of co-dependency unless we have attained self-realization or enlightenment. Our shadow attributes, which all of us have as human beings form our co-dependent nature. Most of us wear social masks to conform to society's expectations and norms. We live inauthentic lives and have inauthentic relationships with our self and with others. We keep ourselves numb and deceive ourselves into thinking that we are happy, that we are successful and have wonderful relationships.

But our shadow attributes, which manifest as co-dependency tendencies—our addictions, compulsions, denials, obsessions, nagging, whining, screaming, worrying, anxieties, distrust, perfectionism, our constant need to fix people and situations, controlling behaviour and our inability to be in the 'moment'—keep us entangled in our repressed emotional and psychological pain. We sink into the abyss of depression, shame, guilt, denial, deceit, pretences and power struggles in and outside of the home. The traumas or challenges that we undergo in childhood and the negative beliefs we hold of ourselves keep us tied to our co-dependent behaviour patterns until we allow the grace of awareness, understanding, acceptance and healing to transform our beliefs and old patterns of behaviour.

There are many books on co-dependent relationships that are available for those who are interested in knowing more about this topic. In Part II, I listed the essential characteristics that are absent in abusive relationships. In this section, I list below some features that define a healthy and authentic partnership in order to distinguish it from a co-dependent relationship and also to point readers towards the kind of relationships towards which we should aspire.

Authenticity, the Key to a Conscious Relationship

Authentic living demands that what we think, believe and feel must be congruent with how we live our lives. If we truly believe we are powerful, then we must feel and embrace the energy of power within us and live our life in ways that reflect that power. The congruency of our inner truth that comes from our true Self must be maintained in all three areas for authenticity to prevail. Before we can form an authentic relationship with another person, we have to be authentic to ourselves. This requires us to go inward to connect with our true Self and to operate from a space where we can remove our social masks in order to live with honesty and integrity. In doing so, the congruency that we establish within us can then be extended into our relationships. In an authentic partnership, both parties are committed to doing their inner work to reconnect with their true Self.

Authentic partnership is a co-operative relationship that encompasses the qualities of mutuality, equality and authenticity**.** As you go through this section, look for the qualities listed below within yourself. Try also to embody the qualities that you would like to see in your partner because the universal law of attraction dictates that you draw the kind of person to you that will mirror what is within you. The following are characteristics of an authentic relationship:

- Equality in the partnership stems from mutuality: mutual love, respect, trust, support, consideration, compassion, open and loving communication, honesty and integrity.

- A partnership based on equality suggests that equal status is enjoyed by both parties in the relationship. The partners are equally involved in decision-making and perceive each other as team-mates. They contribute to the relationship financially, emotionally and physically. There is mutual respect, support and acknowledgement for each other's work, even if the work is to manage the home.

- In an authentic partnership, both parties are free to voice out their preferences and to make choices that are right for them and for the relationship. In instances where conflicts arise, they are able to communicate their feelings and opinions openly and honestly and to constantly forgive each other. At times when emotions run high, they are not afraid to express themselves and to take time out to cool off before attempting to deal with the conflict. They feel secure to be themselves and to bare their souls without fear of being attacked, criticized and belittled. They have no need to assume roles and masks and to pretend to be other than themselves. They love and accept each other for who they are while appreciating their differences.

- The partners strive to be authentic within themselves and in their partnership by trying to work through their issues or self-dividedness. Problems in the relationship are perceived as opportunities to look within themselves and to learn about aspects of themselves. There is the understanding that relationships with others are a mirror of our own inner state of mind and that at the core of all problems is conflict and dividedness within the self. With that understanding in mind, the partners have no need to participate in the blame game and to assume the role of victim or perpetrator. In other words, it is not a 'me versus you' relationship; it is not an 'I've got to be better than you' relationship. It is about looking within one's self and understanding where you and your partner are coming from and working towards restoring harmony within yourself and in your partnership.

- An authentic partnership is one that moves away from a fear-based relationship of power, control and domination, which characterises a co-dependent relationship to one that is soul-based. It is a partnership that fosters emotional connectedness, bonding and intimacy. The partners make an effort in the face of conflict, to turn towards each other and retain their emotional connection. There is deep and genuine caring from the heart, a desire to understand and to relate to one's partner at a deeper and more intimate level.

- Reverence for the partnership that they have created is highlighted as they strive to be true to themselves and to the partnership. Even as they prioritize their relationship, they are not afraid to negotiate their wants and needs to grow as individuals and as partners. They are able to give and receive as cooperation, sharing and harmony are manifest in their relationship. Both parties are willing to carry full responsibility for nurturing and developing the partnership. They are also committed to supporting each other's personal and spiritual growth as they know that these are important elements for happiness in the relationship.

- There is a tendency for the partners to look for commonality and unity to strengthen and deepen their relationship rather than focus on what is wrong with it and how to fix it. They deal with problems as they arise, yet do not focus continually on them. They try not to be reactionary. They do not constantly revert to past mistakes nor react to external triggers but are instead willing to listen and respond in a calm and mature way. Differences of opinions and perspectives are ironed out with due respect and consideration rendered to each other's point of view or with a mutual agreement to disagree. As such, authentic partners will not allow their relationship to become a battleground. Conflicts are handled with the understanding that differences are bound to occur in a relationship as they recognize each other as individuals. Mutual love, honour, respect, consideration, support, negotiation and forgiveness are the reigning elements that sustain authentic partnerships.

Developing an authentic relationship with one's self and with others is a lifelong process. Relationships often throw up challenges as opportunities for us to be present, to grow and to release old patterns of behaviour. Ultimately, we are responsible for the kind of lives we lead. It is dysfunctional to rely on anyone else other than ourselves to fill the emptiness or lack that is within us.

As long as we do not heal this vacuum within us, we will operate from a space of dysfunction and inauthenticity and invite dysfunctional people and situations into our lives. The onus thus lies with us to transcend our negative conditioning and experiences to rewrite life stories that are based on authenticity. In doing so, we should ask ourselves if we have the courage to live the kind of life we want, to speak and walk our truth, and to live our dreams. Or are we compromising to the extent that we are forgoing our truths and dreams for others?

We are faced with choices every moment of our lives and whatever choice we exercise must make us comfortable and at peace. Choices that are made out of fear and anxiety often do not lead to right action.

The choices we make must thus awaken us to our self-respect, self-worth and inner power, of who we are in ourselves and not who we are in the eyes of society.

Chapter 18

Man becomes whole when the conscious and the unconscious is integrated.

Carl Jung

Inner Work: The Integration of the Conscious and Unconscious Mind

The healing of our fragmented selves into wholeness necessitates the integration of the conscious and the unconscious mind. It aids in the unblocking, recovering and transcending of the divided self. The healing practices listed in this chapter are holistic in nature in that they integrate the body, mind and soul. Studies show that physical and emotional illnesses are the manifestation of emotional dysfunction. It is therefore important to embrace a holistic approach that looks beyond just the symptomatic causes of our dysfunction, and take into consideration all aspects of healing. This includes recognizing the essential need to release the past in order to live fully in the present. Ultimately, this mode of being will enable us to not only realize our true Self, it will also help us to develop and access our inner resources, while facilitating access to deeper levels of wisdom, creativity and potentiality.

Though some of these tools may seem like common sense, it is important to note that when one is in a state of utter disarray, overwhelmed by depression and apathy, it takes gargantuan effort to participate in self-care. As such, it becomes necessary for us to incorporate at least some of these practical tools into our daily activities to augment our healing process. Some of the practices overlap and are most effective when practiced together.

Healing Practices

- Self-Inquiry
- Journaling
- Energy Healing through Recapitulation
- Prayer
- Meditation/Observing silence
- Affirmations
- Visualization
- Breathwork
- Bodywork
- Physical Exercise
- Nutrition
- Being in Nature
- Creative work

Self-Inquiry

Healing involves dealing with our shadow self, which necessitates that we soul-search through the techniques of self-inquiry and self-reflection. These are essential tools that lead to self-awareness and clarity. They play a very important part in my personal and spiritual growth as they provide me with clearer insight of myself and show me how to proceed along my life journey.

Self-Inquiry is an ancient technique, derived from a form of meditation practice that traces the root of your thoughts to the I-thought: Who am I? The process entails looking within to explore our motives, attitudes, belief systems, feelings and actions in order to gain a new perspective and better understanding of ourselves. By raising pertinent questions and by reflecting or meditating on them, we gain powerful answers and insights. For instance, in order to heal we may need to know where our sense of unworthiness comes from. Perhaps something was said or done in our childhood or in later years that made us feel bad about ourselves. Or sometimes we may think of ourselves as compassionate, loving and funny and yet behave in ways that are manipulative, arrogant, egocentric or self-indulgent. The incongruence in what we think of ourselves and how we behave is because we have yet to acknowledge our shadow self. Unless we claim and heal our shadow attributes, integrating and balancing them with our light attributes, we will remain powerless and stagnant to initiate change in our life.

Self-inquiry requires us to review what has transpired in our life from an objective point of view rather than from a perspective of guilt, shame or blame if we want healing and growth to take place. It is the awareness of our choices, beliefs and attitudes that will help us to transcend our challenges.

Although shadow work has many layers to it, much healing nevertheless can take place by identifying our core shadow attributes, as I shared in Chapter 16. It would be preferable to combine the practice of self-inquiry with journaling as writing down our feelings, thoughts, goals and plans can be extremely illuminating and cathartic. Furthermore, writing down our self-observations leaves a marked effect on the conscious and subconscious mind, hastening the healing and manifestation process.

The exercises in Chapters 13, 15 and 17, if done diligently, would have helped you to identify your beliefs, attitudes and emotions and to assess the state of your relationship. In this section, we continue with more exercises, incorporating into them the practice of visualization.

EXERCISE

To ascertain the root causes of your emotional pain, you need to:

- Identify your core beliefs, emotions and behaviour patterns that are erroneous. Observe your thoughts and belief system and how they influence your interaction with yourself and with others. You may want to close your eyes and visualize scenarios from your past to identify any event, persons or words used which have caused you pain. Ask yourself what you felt in those moments.
- Raise questions that are pertinent to you. You may want to refer to Chapter 17 for some of the questions that I had raised for myself that may be of relevance to you.
- Here are further examples of questions that you can ask yourself:
- What do I feel about myself?
- What do I feel about others?
- How do I behave when I am on my own and with others?
- What do I believe about love?
- What do I believe about relationships?
- What does success mean to me?
- Is money important to me?

- How have my beliefs created problems for me?
  For example, if you keep having problems at work and in all your personal relationships, ask yourself what belief you are holding in your thought pattern that is creating such a problem. More often than not, our problems are derived from the belief of 'not being good enough.' If you grew up with the belief that money is the root of all evil, then you are most likely not going to enjoy financial success because you are not comfortable receiving it. You will sabotage all opportunities to bring it into your life. Fear of success can also manifest as procrastination in doing one's work or performing well at an interview. Similarly, if you believe that nobody loves you or appreciates you, then you are bound to feel unworthy of receiving love because you are unable to invite people into your life. A friend of mine told me that she believes that nobody will want her if she does not have the 'perfect body.' These are limiting beliefs that sabotage our desire to be happy and must be released.
- Next, be aware of what you are feeling in any situation and ask yourself:
- What emotions do I feel when I think of a certain event or person?
- Do I feel sad, angry, enraged, depressed, jealous, hurt, anxious, abandoned, rejected, lonely, downtrodden, belittled, disregarded, stupid, inadequate, unattractive, violated or fearful?
- Why do I feel angry, sad, depressed, stupid, belittled? Is it because I think that nobody loves me or I feel unappreciated or I feel that I am not good enough?
- Who am I angry with? Myself, my mother, my husband, my teacher?
- Do I have the abandoned child, wounded child, warrior, queen, victim and prostitute archetypes within me?
- How do these sub-personalities affect the way I behave?
- Do I betray myself in order to please others?
- In what ways do I betray myself?

- How do I perceive myself?
- What expectations do I have for myself?
- What do I want from my relationship/s?
- What do I want from life?
- What is important to me?
- Do I feel fulfilled as a person?
- What needs to be changed and healed to make me feel more fulfilled?
- How can I be true to myself?
- How can I move on from the space that I am now in?

It is only by probing deeply into our emotional self and bringing into consciousness what has long been repressed in our subconscious mind through mental garbage spring cleaning that we will be able to move forward to heal the wounds we have sustained.

Journaling

As a self-exploratory tool, journaling is an important technique that is beneficial in emotional healing. It allows us to identify and express our emotions, thoughts, feelings, responses and reactions to attitudes, behaviour patterns and events from an objective and oftentimes more compassionate perspective. Journaling offers us a chance to release repressed emotions and thoughts, disentangle confusion, correct misperceptions and erroneous judgment and identify choices and beliefs that arise from flawed perspectives and attitudes.

EXERCISE

- Once you have identified your erroneous beliefs, habits and attitudes through the process of self-inquiry, choose two of the limiting beliefs or emotions that you would like to work through first and write these down in your journal.

- If anger is an issue with you as it was for me, the first question you should ask yourself is: Why am I angry? What is it that is making me angry? What are the beliefs that I hold which are contributing to my anger in this situation? For me, it was my expectation of having a 'happy and united family.' Always raise questions and keep probing deeper and deeper until you gain a better understanding of your issue.

- Trace the root cause of your anger by reflecting on your past, starting from events in your childhood that may have triggered your anger issues and work your way to the present.

- Then, see if you can relate your anger to your current situation as I did in the previous chapter in analysing my issue of abandonment with my mother and Steven.

- Observe the emotions that surface. The purpose of this exercise is not to accuse and to blame the people who have caused you pain. Neither is it to berate yourself. It is to gain insight into your situation, behaviour and attitude so that you can heal and transform yourself in order to transcend your challenges. It is essential that you deal with the anger constructively instead of repressing it or expressing it violently. An important element of self-growth is self-mastery, which is the power to control one's actions, impulses or emotions.

- Write down the reasons why you are angry. Is it because your expectations are not met: things are not falling into place the way you want them to or because people are not responding and behaving in the way you desired? Is your anger due to a perception of being treated unfairly? Is it because your needs are not being met? If so, write down how you think you are being treated unfairly or in what ways your needs are not being met. It is important that you ascertain the factors that contribute to your anger issue. Anger often stems from dissatisfaction, discontentment and unfulfilled desires, needs and expectations. You need to trace the origins of your anger in order to determine the reason for your unhappiness and to ascertain whether your responses are appropriate, inappropriate, constructive or destructive. It is ultimately awareness that initiates conscious choices and change. You cannot change what you are not aware of.

- Set strategies and goals to deal with your anger. Every time you start feeling angry, be conscious of what is happening to you emotionally and physically, pause and take a deep breath before responding. If you are unable to respond calmly, then it is best to take time out and avoid confrontation until you are ready to talk to the person concerned or to deal with the problem. These are ways in which you can practice being mindful of how you behave.

- Practicing meditation and cultivating inner contentment, patience and peace of mind are antidotes to anger. These are some of the steps that you can implement as part of your goal. No matter what your problem is, you must deal with the issue. Analysing and re-evaluating the thoughts that triggered the anger can help to dissipate it.

- Make a list of things that are not working in your home life, work life, social life, and in your finances. Look deeply and honestly at what is in your thoughts and the belief system that has invited these negative experiences into your life. What you believe of yourself and of life in general is what will be manifested in your life. So, pay close attention to your thoughts and beliefs.

- Take one belief or emotion to work on at a time. Try not to get overwhelmed or daunted by initiating too many changes at one time. It's okay to take small steps. The important thing is to keep working on them and not to give up. Always bear in mind that change, a better life, and growth are in your hands. It is you who has to act on effecting change in your life.

The self-knowledge and awareness that we glean from looking inward will provide us with the clarity to exercise more conscious choices as we focus and clarify our needs, desires, goals and plans. It is however important to note that journaling about negative emotions and events alone, without looking at things from an alternative and more positive perspective, without incorporating reflective thoughts, plans, actions and goals can be detrimental to one's mental health. Focusing exclusively on the negative will not only keep us stagnant but will create more stress and more of these painful and self-destructive experiences in our lives.

Journaling provides opportunities to view past experiences through an alternative, more empowering perspective. Through it, we find the language to think anew about our life. It is crucial that we include positive thoughts, affirmations and alternative plans for actions in our journal to change what is not working for us. It is also necessary for us to review our goals and plans periodically to ascertain that we are growing in the direction we want to take.

Energy Healing Through Recapitulation

Recapitulation is a healing process that requires us to revisit our past, starting from childhood. It offers us opportunities to attain insight into the causes of our pain. It is a beneficial tool that involves energy work. Healing always takes place at an inner energy level first before it is manifested externally. Our emotions are energy like everything else. We transmit energetic frequencies with our focused thoughts, beliefs and feelings. By recapitulating and transmuting our past memories through the processes of meditation and visualization, we can transcend the energy of our painful past.

EXERCISE

- Find a quiet place and close your eyes. Breathe deeply and comfortably until you feel calm and relaxed. Let go of all the tension from your body. As you focus on your breath, breathing deeply from your abdomen, visualize yourself revisiting your childhood.

- Try to recollect your earliest possible memories of any painful or traumatic events that took place in your life, starting from childhood. You may want to begin chronologically from age three to seven. As you scan through those years, wait for any memories, visions or flashes to emerge. If there are none, move on to ages 8-15, 16-25, 26-32 and so forth until you reach your current age. It is best to do it in a chronological order so as to trace the sequence of events that may have shaped your current life experiences.

- At each stage of your recapitulation, allow memories, words, scenes or incidents to surface as you observe or witness what is happening, just like you would in a movie. Try not to judge what you see or hear. Avoid all internal commentary. Instead, allow yourself to feel the emotion that surfaces within you as you recall these incidents. This is an important part of the healing process. Take note of what the pain feels like. Where does it hurt when you feel the emotion of anger or sadness? Do you feel a sense of constriction in your heart or in your stomach or maybe you feel the pain as tension in your shoulders or neck? Be conscious of your bodily sensations and emotions without your mind going into overdrive to make up stories about them.

- Be with the emotion as long as you can, breathing deeply and consciously as you stay with the emotion. Then give the intent to release it to the universe. By not identifying with your pain, you are allowing it to be what it is. Try to accept that these events or incidents took place a long time ago and that the people who have hurt you had done the best they could, given their own past experiences, wounds, vulnerabilities and limitations. Difficult as it may be, try to understand that they were operating from a space of pain that had made them behave in an unconscious manner. By releasing the pain to the universe, you are allowing forgiveness to wash over you.

- Focus on your heart, breathe deeply and allow feelings of love to emanate from your heart. This process allows you to connect with your true Self. Then, give the intent to sincerely forgive the person for what he or she has done to you. Bear in mind that you are forgiving the person and not the act.

- It is necessary that you forgive yourself too. Forgiving allows you to heal and to move forward with your life. It releases you and the other person from the painful bondage.

- Send the person love from your heart. Visualize the energy of love as pure white light flowing from your heart to the other person's heart. The energy envelops the sender and the receiver in a circle of energy that breaks through boundaries and limitations. The purpose of this practice is to generate compassion, forgiveness and healing. Do it often over a period of time.

- The practice of sending love from the heart, together with visualization and prayer, is a powerful healing technique that I often use on myself and on others, especially those who are emotionally and physically in pain. Keep in mind that when you engage in this practice, the energy that you transmit from your heart is love. And love comes from God, from the grace that flows within you. Utilizing love is a powerful force that we can use to harness the inherent goodness in us. It is therefore important to connect to your heart in order to do this practice. Always seek divine guidance in forgiving the people who have hurt you and visualize yourself being set free from the shackles of your past.

- You can also try visualizing yourself in dialogue with the person who has hurt you and with your sub-personalities: your wounded child, victim and critical parent archetypes.

- Switching roles with the other person or sub-personality can also be useful in helping you to see things from a different perspective. You will be surprised by the discernment and wisdom attained in these moments. It is always best to do the energy healing and forgiving process separately for each person, sub-personality or incident that has caused you pain and trauma.

Energy healing through the process of recapitulation thus provides us with the opportunity to change the frequency of our thought patterns, which will inevitably lead to healing and transcending of our painful experiences.

Prayer

I cannot express enough the importance of prayer in the healing process. Call it what you will, prayer is in reality, simply talking or connecting with God or a Higher Power or Higher Intelligence, sincerely from our heart for the "Kingdom of heaven" is within us. We can talk to God wherever we are and in whatever circumstances, in moments of happiness or in sadness. God is present everywhere. God is spirit. God is energy. And God resides in each and every one of us.

As we pray or communicate with God, we learn to listen to God's voice through the silence in our hearts, where God resides in us as spirit. It is within this inner space that we experience God and the oneness of spirit as we connect with our true Self. Healing progresses well if we are receptive to divine grace and allow it to work in our lives. Through prayer, we can experience the presence of God in us as love, peace, compassion, contentment and joy.

Prayer is, without doubt, the most powerful healing tool that is also life transforming. Prayer is an act of faith. Research conducted by world renowned scientists and verified by investigative journalist and author of **The Field**, Lynne McTaggart, shows that patients with terminal illnesses, including those at the end stage of their illness, improved tremendously in health when others prayed for them despite not being informed of the supplication. The studies note that the intercessors had wholeheartedly believed that a Higher Power or God would respond to their prayers to heal the person being prayed for. This shows that it is faith that biochemically affects every cell in the body to activate the potential for healing to take place.

Even a simple feeling of gratitude for what we have in our life can do wonders to initiate the process of healing since gratitude encompasses prayer. When I was six years old, I asked my father how I should pray. Even though I was taught to pray as a young girl, prayer had seemed to me like a mechanical recitation of Thanksgiving. I did not feel the connection from my heart until my father told me one day,

"Just talk to God. Tell Him what is in your heart. He's always listening to us."

God listens to our prayers and works miracles in our lives, which are often passed off as mere coincidence to those who do not believe in a Higher power working in their lives. There are no coincidences. God is always there for us if we allow him into our lives. God knows what is in our hearts. All we have to do is to talk to Him, to connect with Him and He will work through us to effect the change that we need to precipitate healing.

Transformation often occurs when there is a change in mind-set. When we change our thoughts, beliefs and attitudes, we change our consciousness, which puts forth into motion a change in our circumstances. It is absolute faith and trust in God's healing power that allows divine grace to restore our broken spirit and provide us with the steadfastness and courage required to transcend our adversities.

Meditation

Meditation, or 'observing silence,' as some prefer to call it, is another important tool that I have used on a daily basis as part of my healing and spiritual practice. Meditation entails engaging in deep contemplation, which fosters non-judgmental awareness by connecting us to our true or Higher Self. Meditation allows us to listen to the still voice of God within the sacred space of our heart.

So while prayer involves talking to God, meditation is about listening to God. Meditation reveals revelation by Spirit that some call intuition and others, divine guidance. The practice allows divine grace to fill us with inner peace and provide us with the clarity, wisdom and power to exercise conscious choices. It is within this inner space of our heart that healing takes place, where insight is gleaned and our true Self is accessed. It is also here that the awareness of the unity and the interconnectedness of human beings is realized, which develops our compassion for fellow human beings and grows our desire to alleviate others' suffering.

Practicing meditation deeply and consistently develops in us a kind of self-awareness or mindfulness and inner strength that assist us in transcending the storms in our lives, sparing us the debilitating and devastating effects of upheaval and overwhelm. The practice of meditation allows us to accept and to cope with the current situation, enabling us to make decisions from a better space. It is about surrendering to the life event and not demanding that things be other than what it is. In letting go of expectation of what cannot be changed such as a recalcitrant errant partner as we saw in Tessa's case, by releasing obsessive self-recriminations and clinging, one is able to move forward to a space of inner peace and grace to change one's circumstances without the debilitating effects of overwhelm. Meditation is therefore not just about being quiet; neither is it about the absence of challenges. It is about being the witness, the observer of one's life's experiences. It is about transcending the ego self that thrives on drama, pain and suffering.

Physiologically, meditation generates health benefits as it involves conscious breathing. Meditation develops concentration and promotes deep relaxation, with the brain emitting alpha and theta waves. These waves have the power to calm the mind, relax the body, and balance and harmonize the discordant energies within us. Other benefits also include increased perceptiveness, creativity and a greater sense of well-being. Meditation, especially when done with visualization, enhances greatly the transformative powers of healing and manifestation in our lives.

Meditation helped me tremendously to calm my agitated emotions. It helped me to release my anger, pain and tension through focused breathing. Sometimes, meditation brought to the surface painful events from the past. By being with the pain and observing past events as a witness, I was able to release the pain to the universe. I had different reactions at different times. There have been times in the early stages of my healing journey when I have burst into tears when scenarios with my mother emerged, offering me the opportunity to heal and to release repressed emotions. At other times, I have viewed these events with detachment. They have often provided me with the opportunity to view events from an alternative perspective.

Meditation thus offers a new way to view the same phenomenon. We often make assumptions, associations and judgments to give meaning to our experiences. These meanings are derived from norms, expectations and habits that have been ingrained in us since young. Although these value judgments may not always be logical, yet they are accepted as 'truths' because we have been conditioned to think in a certain way. Meditation breaks down these assumptions through the act of observing. As an observer, we are able to stand back to watch ourselves and the events in our lives objectively. This helps us to dis-identify with our thoughts. A thought is then viewed as being merely a thought. Any emotion attached to it is released. In the process, we become aware that we are not our stories. From this point of detachment, we can arrive at choices that are right for us. Meditation therefore enables us to attain inner peace so that no matter what goes on in our lives, we will remain unshakeable. The journey to selfhood is a life long process that requires effort, time and patience.

EXERCISE

- Find a quiet place away from all distraction.
- Sit comfortably on a chair in an upright position, keeping your spine straight.
- Close your eyes and relax.
- Breathe in slowly and deeply as you relax your body.
- Focus on each part of your body as you release the tension from your muscles.
- Breathe through your nose and not through your mouth.
- When you inhale, the abdomen should rise first followed by the chest.
- When you exhale, the chest should descend first before the abdomen.
- As you breathe in and out, keep your focus on the air entering the nostrils, the abdomen and the rising of the chest.

- Do the same for the outflow.
- As your breathing becomes more comfortable and fluid, observe any thought or image that may arise. Release any inclination to build up stories around it.
- Let the thought or image pass and return your focus to your breathing.
- Stay in that state until you are ready to end the meditation

You will feel refreshed and calm after the practice. Whenever you feel angry or agitated, try to meditate because silence is the bridge to peace and stillness. You may want to start off meditating for 10-15 minutes, or less if you find it difficult to concentrate. It gets easier as you progress. I personally like to meditate with soft instrumental music in the background although I practice silent and walking meditation too. I find that the vibration from the music helps me to enter a deep meditative state. Please refer to the end of this section for the exercise on energy healing meditation, which you may want to attempt as you get more comfortable with the meditation practice.

Affirmation

Like prayer, affirmation involves belief. Every thought we have of ourselves, of someone or something, be it positive or negative, is an affirmation. Since our thoughts become our reality, what we feed into our subconscious mind through our habitual self-talk not only becomes an integral part of the perception we hold of ourselves, it also influences our behaviour.

To effect transformation through affirmation, we need to regulate our negative self-talk by first discerning the root causes of our problems, whether it be fear, lack of confidence, poor self-image or addictive habits. Every time someone says, "I can't do it," "I don't have the courage to do it," or "I am not smart enough to do it," she reinforces those beliefs. Since the brain believes what it is ingrained with, the belief then becomes a self-fulfilling prophecy, with the person behaving exactly in ways that reinforces her self-talk and self-image.

Underlying the negative belief is often the fear of not being good enough, which is the root cause of most of our problems. Positive change can be effected by tracing the event that precipitated the fear via meditation and visualization, and then following this up with positive affirmations and visualization. The power of the imagination to reprogram the subconscious mind is immeasurable when done with faith and consistency.

Affirmations should be specifically formulated to program a desired emotion or behaviour into your subconscious mind. If you want to instil self-confidence or self-esteem for instance, you will have to:

EXERCISE

- Formulate positive affirmations such as "I am confident," "I am intelligent," "I am competent," "I am grateful," "I am attractive," "All is well in my world." Take one affirmation to work on first. You can write these affirmations in your journal or on cards or on your vision board. These affirmations generate a sense of well-being that starts the flow for change to occur in the psyche.
- Feeling the emotion behind the affirmations is crucial in the manifestation process. You have to feel the confidence flowing in you. You have to feel the expectancy of being a certain way. For the transformation to take place in your psyche, studies show that it is crucial for you to actually feel the emotion behind the belief.
- Fuel the belief with passion and excitement. Engaging your emotion generates the energy for the desired result.
- Next, imagine yourself as confident, as intelligent, as competent.
- Then, visualize the achieved reality or outcome, such as seeing yourself acting confident at a board meeting.
- Keep editing negative thoughts as they arise and change them to positive affirmations.

- Finally, start acting as if you are confident. Start speaking up and reaching out to others if the normal tendency is for you to keep quiet. Take small steps to build up your confidence by pushing yourself to do things beyond your comfort zone. Every step you take will help you to grow in ways you never thought you would.

There is no doubt that changing negative habits and your self-image takes determination and persistence, but done consistently over a period of time, these exercises have been proven to reap benefits. According to Joshua David Stone, author of *Soul Psychology*, and Dr. Joseph Murphy, author of *Power of Your Subconscious Mind*, it takes at least 21 days of diligent and consistent work to reprogram the subconscious mind. The 21 days and thereafter of reprogramming our subconscious mind will get us into the habit of not only perceiving ourselves in a more positive way but also in behaving that way because the new image and belief that we hold of ourselves will eventually become our reality.

Visualization

Visualization goes hand in hand with affirmation. To visualize is to create a mental picture or to imagine vividly what we want in our life in terms of self-image, goals, dreams and achievements. Visualization is a very powerful tool that many successful people such as Napoleon Hill, Albert Einstein, and Andrew Carnegie as well as CEOs and athletes have used to achieve their desired goals and dreams. Most of us engage in visualization daily without even realizing it. We think of the things that we want to do on a daily basis and hold images of how to carry them out in our minds.

However, prolonged visualization is needed to change negative habits, attitudes and beliefs. Like affirmation, visualization uses the power of focused thought and belief to physically change a situation. Because thoughts have energetic frequencies, the thoughts we hold of ourselves and of our life are sent out to the universe and mirrored back to us through events, situations and relationships. Since our emotions play an integral part in our belief system, it is essential that we hold positive images and thoughts of what we want to manifest in our lives. If we wholeheartedly believe in our mind that a healing or a desired result has already occurred, it increases the success of their physical manifestation.

Masaru Emoto's book *The Messages from Water* discusses experiments that showed that beautiful music as well as gratitude, positive affirmations and visualizations directed at a certain quantity of water such as a glass of water, positively impacted on its molecular composition. The positive energetic frequencies created beautiful crystal patterns in the water. Similarly, Emoto's research showed that negative energetic frequencies transmitted through anger, hatred and sorrow impacted the composition of water by creating distortions in the formation of the water crystals.

Interestingly, there is increasing scientific evidence to show that Emoto's findings hold true for our physical bodies as well: positive and negative energetic frequencies of our thoughts and emotions can impact the cellular structure of our physical body and affect the state of our overall health. We can discern from these findings how the power of our thoughts and emotions can affect not only us and our relationships but also our environment and the planet.

When we combine prayer with positive affirmations, visualization, meditation and appropriate action, we inevitably ignite the innate power within us to transform our lives.

EXERCISE

- Using the tool of recapitulation, go back to your childhood and think of all the images you have carried of yourself.
- If any of them are negative, for e.g. if you thought of yourself as fat, stupid, ugly, or incompetent, you need to change these images.
- Reformulate new positive images of yourself.

- If you start carrying positive images of yourself as confident, intelligent, or lovable, these will be reflected back to you over time. You need to hold better images of yourself and believe in them.
- Monitor your thoughts and images. Always ask yourself what energy you are putting out there.
- Reinforce the positive images with verbal and written affirmations. Do this daily until it is integrated into your subconscious mind and you start seeing yourself in a new light. You might find this exercise uncomfortable to do at first but if you want to see changes in your life, you need to be determined and keep practicing.

Because all our habits, attitudes and past memory are controlled by our subconscious mind, we need to filter what we will allow into our mind. We need to be aware of negative images and beliefs derived from cultural and religious ideological systems that may have limited us as a person. This includes buying into stereotypical gender roles of what defines a man or woman. We should never live other people's script for us. Instead, we should write our own script of what we would like to see changed in ourselves and in our life. Prayer, affirmations, visualization and changing how we talk about ourselves internally and to others are the fastest ways to release old patterns of behaviour.

Breathwork

The breath is the source of life. Breathwork is sacred to many traditions. It goes hand in hand with meditation and is sometimes used in psychotherapy. Breathwork involves utilizing the healing and transformative powers of deep conscious breathing. Yoga and Tai chi are some of the ancient practices that make use of conscious and focused deep breathing. Conscious breathing is the bridge between the mind and body. It connects us to our inner world, to the life force that flows within us. This life force or energy is referred to as *Prana* in Sanskrit while the Chinese refer to it as the *Chi or Tao*. Conscious breathing or meditation allows the energy in our body to flow smoothly through our energy centres, also called the **Meridian points** by the Chinese and **Chakras** in Sanskrit, to remove any energetic blockages that manifest as emotional and physical pain.

Conscious breathing anchors us in the present moment. It raises our energetic vibration and inevitably connects us to our higher consciousness, thereby creating increased awareness. When we focus on our breath, it silences our very often overly active mind, paving the way for understanding and clarity. Because it enables us to be connected with the life force within us, conscious breathing creates a sense of aliveness and greater energy as it invigorates the body.

In contrast, breathing patterns that are shallow and fast are often the result of a stressful and fast-paced lifestyle. There are some people who are so stressed out that they have been known to stop breathing momentarily. Poor breathing inevitably affects the quality of life. Stress and tension constrict the heart and impede the flow of energy in the body. We release tension from the body without realizing it when we sigh: this is a natural phenomenon to compensate for the lack of deep breathing. We expand our heart when we experience beauty and joy. Have you noticed that there is a natural tendency for us to take a deep breath when we are happy or when we stand in awe of something beautiful?

Practicing conscious breathing is thus a good way to release stress and tension. It improves the quality of life as the breath is connected to the nervous system. Conscious breathing activates inner healing and cleanses the organs, glands and cells. It improves the circulation of oxygen and nutrients to the body, thereby revitalizing the entire system. Any blockages of energy in the body, which manifest as negative emotional patterns and pain, are released through conscious breathing. By visualizing and breathing energy into these areas of blockages in our body, we can dissolve pain and release negative emotions and thoughts. Conscious breathing is a lifestyle change that confers spiritual and health benefits. It promotes deep relaxation and peace of mind while regulating our moods and connecting us to our true Self.

Bodywork

Bodywork involves any form of massage therapy and skeletal manipulation. There are different forms of bodywork: acupressure, Rolfing, deep tissue massage, *tui na*, a form of Chinese manipulative therapy that works with the energy system in the body just like acupressure and acupuncture, reflexology and lymphatic massage, among others. Bodywork is a form of therapeutic treatment and has healing effects. It is beneficial for those who have undergone deep trauma or emotional pain that has manifested in their physical and emotional bodies as energetic blockages and physical illnesses. Bodywork helps to release these energetic blockages that have become embedded in the deep tissues, muscles and skeletal system. It releases stress, nervous tension and pain as endorphins are released into the circulatory system. Bodywork is an important part of self-care and love that one can give to oneself, the healing touch of human hands.

Physical Exercise

Exercise is another form of self-care and love that we can give to ourselves. Since the physical body houses our spirit or soul, taking care of it becomes just as important as taking care of our emotional body. This is particularly so for those of us who have experienced abuse and trauma as there is a tendency for us to be embroiled in waves of depression and apathy. Engaging in physical exercise keeps us from wallowing in self-pity and from focusing on our pain. Exercise allows us instead to be focused on the present moment, so that it is in itself, meditative.

Physical exercise confers emotional and health benefits. Socially, exercise is a depression buster as it creates opportunities for social interaction. Emotionally, exercise increases motivation and self-esteem; it also aids in alleviating apathy and stress by producing serotonin, a happy hormone that uplifts moods. Endorphins, a group of hormones that are released during physical activity, interact with the receptors in the brains to reduce the perception of pain while increasing a sense of well-being. Physically, exercise improves the immune system, which is often lowered by depression, and strengthens the physical body.

Spending Time in Nature

Spending time in nature offers therapeutic value. Nature is food for the soul. Research has shown that there is faster recovery from stress in response to stimuli from nature than from urban settings. Being in nature strengthens the immune system, reduces stress hormones, lowers blood pressure and improves social interaction within group settings. Exercise also helps relieve physical and mental fatigue and increases overall well-being and vitality due to the negative ions released from the natural surroundings. Negative ions balance the hormone serotonin in the body. This is why people feel more alert and energized in the presence of negative ions.

The air near waterfalls, mountains, beaches, lakes and forests are among the places where ionization levels are in complete and natural balance. Thus, engaging in activities such as gardening, hiking, camping, fishing, boating or signing up for farm stays and nature retreats provides us with wonderful opportunities to experience and appreciate nature's beauty. Besides, being in a natural environment not only has a calming effect on us, it helps us to connect with our Creator and thus raises our spiritual vibration. Nature has much to teach us about life. Just observing the rhythms and flows of nature helps us to surrender to the cyclical process of life.

Creative Work

Getting involved in any form of creative work can facilitate our healing process as we focus our attention on nurturing our innate creative abilities. Music, painting, sculpting, pottery, writing, landscaping, designing and scientific invention are some of the creative works that are restorative. Creative work is meditative: it keeps us focused and in the moment. Engaging in any form of creative work generates our innate creativity and helps us to connect with our true Self.

Any form of inspiration that comes from our creative work reflects our connection with the divine source within us. Artists, poets and scientists like Pablo Picasso, William Blake, T.S. Eliot, Albert Einstein, and Carl Jung were highly spiritual people who asserted that their work was not theirs but that it came from a Higher Source. In fact, some of the best creative work has been produced in adversity.

Energy Healing Meditation

EXERCISE

- Find a quiet place to meditate, away from distractions and sounds that might disturb your concentration.
- Sit comfortably on a chair or a cushion and keep your spine straight.
- Close your eyes and breathe slowly but deeply.
- Relax every muscle in your body.
- Feel the tension leave your body as your focus on your breath.
- As you inhale through your nose, feel your abdomen expand.
- As you exhale through your nose, feel your abdomen contract.
- Be conscious of your breathing and keep it slow and rhythmic.
- As you concentrate on your breath, your mind will start to slow down.
- You may notice some tingling sensations and warmth in your body as you feel the energy course through your body.
- Visualize a bright beam of white light flowing through the crown of your head to all parts of your body.
- Now, direct your focus to your heart as you continue to breathe slowly.
- Visualize a bright luminescent light emanating from your heart.
- Allow healing of the heart to take place as you connect with the source of the light in your heart.

- Feel the warmth of the light energy flowing through all the cells in your body, revitalizing and energizing your body, mind and spirit.
- Do not fight too hard to concentrate. Notice any thoughts or emotions that surface, release them and return your focus to your breath until you are ready to end the meditation.

You can start off by focusing on your breath for 10 minutes on a daily basis. Focused or conscious breathing can be done anywhere, while walking or performing daily chores. As you get more comfortable with it, you can proceed to meditate for a longer period of time. Meditation is a time that we give to ourselves to be quiet, to recover and to tap into the universal energy. Through it, we not only experience calm and equanimity but also access our potential to allow creativity, abundance, zest and joy, which are our spiritual birthrights, to flow into our lives.

Alchemy of the 'Sacred Fire', Burning Off the Dross of What Is Inauthentic in Us

The healing and transformational journey to selfhood is an on-going process that requires commitment and diligence. It is about choosing to be conscious at every point of our life, living a life of balance and harmony and celebrating the sacredness of life.

I have come to see my experiences in life as a powerful and learning process that has attuned me to my Higher self. The void that I once felt in my life is now filled with divine grace. I am learning daily to live my truth by loving and accepting myself, by assuming complete responsibility for my choices, for the achievement of my goals, dreams and desires, for my happiness and hence, for the quality of my life.

I have allowed the refining 'sacred fire' to ignite in me the fire of passion to live my life fully. Although there have been times when I have given in to doubt, borne out of lack of trust in the natural unfolding of my life, and faltered, I soon realigned myself, strengthened by the lessons offered by the digressions.

Life makes allowances for us to experience and even make errors in our learning. If we can perceive our challenges as opportunities to grow and not allow them to debilitate us, we can move forward in life with more ease and grace. One of the lessons I have learned is that when we actively seek and demand love, it becomes elusive, but the moment we stop seeking love, approval and attention from external sources, love appears in our lives. This simple truth reminded me of the time when my son, John, and his friend had gone hiking to look for a waterfall but ended up going around in circles instead. The more desperate they were to find it, the more elusive it became. After an hour of futile searching, they gave up the idea and decided to enjoy the hike. The moment they decided to let go of seeking the desired waterfall, they found it. It is in the living and enjoying of the present moment that we embrace life.

We often go through the scorching fire of trials and tribulations as a transformational journey to an integrated selfhood. I have come to realize that the more I resist and struggle with life, the more I swim against the currents, the more painful and overwhelming the journey becomes until I am forced to surrender and accept the alchemical fire of transformation.

It takes tremendous effort and courage to confront and to allow the sacred fire to burn away the dross of what is inauthentic in us and in our lives. But as we allow it to refine, purify and mould us, it will dismantle our defences and mental cages and allow love, compassion, forgiveness and grace to flow in our lives. As painful as the re-birthing process of the refining fire is, I believe that it can only pave the way for the birth of a new consciousness, a new self and a new life. For out of the ashes of the flaming forest, sprouts new growth.

Chapter 19

He who is devoid of the power to forgive is devoid of the power to Love. There is some good in the worst of us and some evil in the best of us.

Martin Luther King

Forgiveness: The Power of the Sacred Heart

I was divinely guided not to begin on this chapter on forgiveness until I was able to release myself from the bondage of unforgiveness towards myself and those who have hurt me. Even though I had every intention to forgive Steven, having made the decision to do so even before I had left my marital home, I realized that making the decision to forgive was quite different from forgiving and surrendering completely from the heart.

Each time I had convinced myself that I had forgiven Steven and had felt quite peaceful, something he would say or do (we remain in contact) or some situation would arise to trigger off my pain. My then still reactive behaviour and the bitterness I still felt in those moments made me realize that I had more healing to do to release myself from the pain of unforgiveness.

The writing of this book took a hiatus for about eight months as I worked on myself through all the exercises I mentioned in the previous chapter. I prayed fervently, often seeking guidance, wisdom and clarity while allowing the healing process to take its natural course until I received divine guidance to proceed with the book. I knew that I had more or less released myself from the shackles of hurt and unforgiveness then. Even though it took me some time to get over the grieving and to extricate myself from the excruciating pain of betrayal, I could not but help feel a sense of triumph that I had managed to transcend my past and to move on with my life.

What is Forgiveness?

Forgiveness is the willingness to end resentment, indignation or anger as a result of perceived offence, difference or mistake, and ceasing to demand punishment or restitution (*Oxford English Dictionary*).

Why Forgive?

Spiritual Principle

Most moral, spiritual and religious principles include forgiveness, love and compassion as basic tenets of rightful living. As for me, I grew up with the constant reminder from my father to never hold on to grudges or grievances against another. He often told us that those who were unwilling to forgive only harmed themselves. Although I grew up with this spiritual principle deeply etched in my heart, I nevertheless found it extremely difficult to forgive Steven and Jessica.

I kept reminding myself of what Jesus had taught: that we are to forgive 70x7 times if our brother does us wrong. I was no saint. I was very much a human, with my human foibles and vulnerabilities, just as Steven and Jessica were. Even though we may not find it easy to forgive when we have been broken in spirit and body, it is nevertheless the only way to transcend our painful experience.

As I knew that only forgiveness would set me free, I made the choice to forgive to release myself from the venom of bitterness. Unforgiveness is like an insidious cancer that spreads and consumes us: it kills our zest for life and blocks our creativity, abundance and joy. If we are not careful, the bitterness and resentment that result from unforgiveness may manifest in all of our relationships as cynicism.

I was determined not to allow unforgiveness to ruin my life and to impede my spiritual growth, which was of paramount importance to me. I also knew that only the grace of God working in my life would propel me into the space of love, peace and strength, from which I would be able to forgive. As Marianne Williamson says in her book *A Gift of Change*, "There is no peace without forgiveness." Abiding peace can only come from Spirit that dwells within each and every one of us.

To Transcend the Past

Forgiveness is a choice. It is not a sign of weakness. We do not become doormats by choosing to forgive. In fact, it takes great courage, strength and an open heart to forgive the people who have hurt us deeply. Mahatma Ghandhi said, "The weak cannot forgive: forgiveness is an attribute of the strong."

Forgiveness is of the soul. To forgive is to be vigilant to being in the heart and taking care not to retreat into a fear-based reaction that relies on hatred, revenge and retaliation. It does not, however, mean that we forget the abuse by condoning the acts, take refuge in denial or even make excuses for the perpetrator such as: "that is the way it is," "he is usually this way when he is tired," "it is normal behaviour in our culture," or "he has been abused himself in the past."

To do so would be to deny our right to be treated with respect and dignity. Some women have interpreted the tenet of forgiveness as it is advocated in scriptures to mean long suffering on the part of the wives. As such, they continually forgive their recalcitrant spouses for their errant ways. Condoning abuse is not only sacrilegious to God's love, it perpetuates violence and is a disservice to both the targeted and the perpetrator as both become entwined in a cycle of fear, pain and suffering.

It is essential that we distinguish the person from the act. We acknowledge the transgression but still choose to respond to it with forgiveness and by taking appropriate action to lay down boundaries to curtail it. Forgiveness means moving forward into a space of 'loving thy neighbour as thyself' as scripture decrees in order to transcend the transgression.

Forgiving the person however does not necessarily mean that we have to reconcile with them. For a relationship that is beyond repair or is too destructive, reconciliation may not be the best option. In such a case, we can still choose to forgive the person from afar. The decision to forgive should also not depend on whether the other person acknowledges his behaviour or seeks forgiveness from us.

We choose to forgive regardless of the outcome. It may not lead to reconciled relationships but it definitely leads to healed lives. Although in our pain, we may think that the other person does not deserve to be forgiven, we must understand that forgiveness is, in reality, as much a gift to ourselves as it is a gift to the other because it frees us from our bondage to the past. In forgiving, we attain inner peace.

Forgiveness is therefore a willingness to challenge the obstacles in our lives and to love and honour ourselves. It is a willingness to embrace a spirit of transformation, growth and renewal and is, without doubt, redemptive!

To Heal Body, Mind and Spirit

Extensive research carried out by Dr. Fred Luskin at Stanford University attests to the healing powers of forgiveness. Dr. Luskin suggests that, in addition to its spiritual implications, forgiveness is good for physical and emotional health. His study shows that when we carry repressed destructive feelings of resentment and anger, they eventually manifest in our bodies as physical illnesses and emotional problems.

Holding on to negative emotions is exhaustive and consumes our life. It creates depression and feelings of hopelessness; it affects our immune, cardiovascular and nervous systems by increasing the stress hormones cortisol and adrenaline. In contrast, forgiveness, prayers, faith, trust and inner peace activate healing.

To Restore Inner Freedom

Forgiveness is our ultimate road to inner freedom. It empowers us to dissolve the fetters that shackle us to our past. Forgiveness allows for a new beginning, a rebirth that promotes personal and spiritual growth. Forgiveness is the ultimate tool that restores us to our true Self because forgiveness can only come from a space of unconditional love and compassion.

We attain inner freedom when we can embrace an alternative perspective of our experience. The universal law of attraction dictates that if we allow our lives to be ruled by our fears, negative emotions, self-sabotaging and self-destructive behaviour, we will inevitably create a life of disharmony, pain and suffering. By the same token, if we live in peace, love and joy, these elements are exactly what will be transmitted into every aspect of our life.

Once we are able to comprehend the ramifications underlying the universal law of cause and effect, it will not be difficult for us to see that what we have created in our lives is as it is: what is termed 'imperfect' is, in reality, perfect since we have created the discord in our lives through our own distorted thoughts, beliefs and attitudes. Like love, anger and pain are expressions of our creation. Every decision we make in life stems from either love or fear. Abusive relationships are the result of fear and insecurities residing in our shadow.

Our painful experiences stem from our own ignorance, often derived from a lack of knowledge of our true Self. Hence, from a soul perspective, there are no victims since it is we who have created this reality from our own state of powerlessness. If we hold this perspective in mind, we will be able to forgive ourselves and the people who have hurt us.

Painful and difficult as our experiences may have been, the challenges we face in life often have a purpose in helping us to grow personally and spiritually. Many of us have looked back and realized that the adversities we have gone through have in fact opened doors to new opportunities and beginnings when we took the time to heal ourselves and were receptive to change. To forgive then is to attain the inner freedom to be who we really are.

How do we Forgive?

Be in the Heart

The Zen master, Thick Nhat Hanh aptly said that, "Forgiveness will not be possible until compassion is born in the heart." Compassion occurs when we learn to walk in another person's shoes. It generates a genuine desire to alleviate the other person's suffering. Jesus Christ left us two very significant commands: to love God with all our heart and soul; and to love one another. If we can truly adhere to these two commands, compassion and empathy will assume their natural state in us.

However, it is only in forgiving ourselves that we can extend compassion to others. Often the pain of our experiences makes us close our hearts and become distrustful and defensive. But when we realign ourselves to allow grace to break down the barriers and walls we have constructed around us, forgiving becomes possible. Once I had released the self-recriminations, anger and unforgiveness towards myself, I was able to feel compassion for myself and for Steven.

Compassion arises when we acknowledge our connection with another human being. According to the Dalai Lama, the moment we acknowledge that everyone deserves to be free from suffering, we allow compassion into our lives. Often in our state of pain, it is easy to be dragged into a black hole that can overwhelm and dominate our lives to the point of self-absorption. But when we muster love and gratitude in our lives as the Dalai Lama suggests, we will begin to realize that there are many others who are in the same boat as us, and some are in even worse situations. In this manner, we see the futility of hanging on to our grudges and grievances.

By shifting the focus of our pain to that of others, we learn to shift our perspective of life. We learn to accept that even though some forms of adversity, like happiness, are part and parcel of life, it is ultimately how we choose to respond to our situation, to our trials and tribulations that can either shorten or prolong our suffering.

Let Go of Grievance Stories

The moment we shift our perspective regarding our circumstance and claim back our power through the miracle of forgiveness, we embrace the spirit of redemption. We have the ability to transform our life from a state of limitation and fear to a state of abundance, creativity and love when we replace the attention we give to our grievance stories with positive thoughts, attitudes and beliefs. This, as I have mentioned before, is possible after a period of grieving and healing. Like the Dalai Lama, Dr. Fred Luskin also suggests in his book *Forgive for Good* that we can learn to change the channel of our stories from ourselves to others. Each time we start obsessing about our story, we need to immediately stop and tune it out and turn our focus instead on others.

It is critical for us to understand that while sharing our grievances with friends and therapists can be helpful for a period of time, we need to move on and not identify with our grievance stories. Keep in mind that while we are stuck with our hurt, bitterness and rage, the other party may have moved on with his life. When we rewrite our stories, we empower ourselves; we announce to others that we are important.

Release Blame

Letting go of blame is another important process of forgiveness. To blame is to attack another; it is to make the other person wrong and bad. It constitutes a failure in seeing things from an alternative perspective. Blame attributes everything that has transpired in one's life to others' actions without acknowledging one's own responsibility. It is a refusal to acknowledge that we have the power of choice in how we want our life to unfold and who we want in our space. Acknowledging one's contribution to the dysfunction of the relationship does not exonerate the perpetrator. Abuse in any form, as I continue to reiterate, is a choice. It is a choice based not on love. Love is the only healing power that can bring balance to what is dysfunctional.

Once we acknowledge that life has no guarantees, it releases us from the blame game. Although we may be imbued with expectations of having a faithful partner and a happy and long-lasting relationship, things may not always happen the way we expect them to. It is by clinging on to beliefs and expectations that life should proceed in a certain way or that our partner must behave in a certain manner that we end up imposing, what Dr. Luskin calls 'unenforceable rules' on our partner and our relationship.

One of the unenforceable rules I had stubbornly held on to was the idea of an intact family. But I have since had to challenge my fixed notions of how my world should be. Attempting to enforce rules or expectations where these are unenforceable, as in the case of a recalcitrant philandering partner, is like trying to squeeze water from a stone. It is dysfunctional and harmful to us. It requires that a better choice be exercised instead.

Let Go of Co-Dependency

Our attachment to people, things, and ideas and our expectations and rules motivate our behaviours, habits, thoughts and belief system. Over-attachment, however, is dysfunctional as it creates a reluctance to embrace alternative perceptions. When we become emotionally overdependent on our partner, we are unable to break free and often end up hanging on to our relationship despite its dysfunction.

Relinquishing an unhealthy attachment to our partner, to our grievance stories, to our expectations, anger and unforgiveness, is an important process that inevitably opens us to new possibilities and growth. It frees us from co-dependent behaviour, from seeking love, attention and approval from others, while propelling us into a space of forgiveness and love. As the Buddhist believe, everything will come to pass if we trust in the natural flow of life and revere the many good things we have in our lives. It is gratitude that opens new doors.

Change and growth are therefore natural progressions of life. We are here to understand the self, to expand and experience life in its greatest glory. Our soul is always urging us to greater expressions of ourselves. It is entirely up to us to grasp these possibilities, to enlarge the scope of our horizon and not to limit our potentialities by living in fear of being more than we are.

The Heart is the Key to Embracing Life

The heart is ultimately the gateway of receptivity and compassion. It is the key to life! And life is about expansion: it fuels the power of love within us to heal, to forgive, to respond to life's flow of gratitude, abundance, creativity and joy.

To withhold forgiveness is therefore to withhold love from ourselves. The soul withers as unforgiveness depletes the vital life force that is crucial for living a full and meaningful life. But when we introduce love into the dynamics of any situation or relationship, we invite new and exciting possibilities into our lives because the energy that we put out changes.

To truly love is to live life in the Now moment. It is to be free from the inner dialogue that rules our minds, that obsesses and controls our actions; it is to be free from recriminations of the self and of others, to be free of fear to live, love and to experience life. It is about seizing every moment to be the love that we are and to grasp every opportunity to live life fully with integrity and joy.

Chapter 20

Human Beings and all living things are a coalescence of energy in a field of energy connected to everything in the world. This pulsating energy field is the central engine of our being and our consciousness, the alpha and the omega of our energy body.

Lynne McTaggart

Love: The Greatest Energy Of All

Relationship with Jason

The greatest energy of all is love: its source is derived from our Creator. Love encompasses love for God, love for oneself, love for others and love for life. It is the conduit for a passionate, zestful and fulfilling life. As I healed, I was overtaken by a sense of quietude. The hope that flourished in my heart left me feeling contented as I turned inward to the source of my true Self to love and nurture myself. I felt grateful for my life.

As I surrendered to the flow and goodness of life, I became more receptive to others, embracing them with my love and warmth and accepting theirs in return. It was in this mode of receptivity that Jason walked into my life. I was drawn to his warm, loving and caring energy. Our friendship developed rapidly along the lines of mutual care, love and support.

Jason provides me with the companionship, emotional bonding and nurturing that was lacking in my previous relationship. For the most part of our interaction, we are able to communicate our needs without fear of ridicule and discuss issues and problems as they arise. As mirrors to each other's shadow self, our interactions have occasionally brought to surface the vulnerabilities of our unresolved hurts for healing. Jason and I find that praying together when conflicts arise between us helps to ease the tension and to keep the love for each other flowing. Our disagreements have often provided us with the impetus to communicate our feelings and to grow as individuals and as partners.

There will always be challenges for us to deal with but what is important is how we respond and address them. Often, conflicts in a relationship or situation provide us with the opportunity to learn about ourselves: our weaknesses illuminate the areas we need to work on. The purpose of our sojourn on earth is to learn and grow from our experiences, to develop relationships with ourselves and with others that are wholesome. Every situation or encounter, whether positive or negative, offers us an opportunity to be aware of how we can expand our potential to embrace wholeness. It is within our ability to keep transcending our challenges by constantly keeping our hearts open, even when the inclination is to close it for fear of getting hurt that enables us to move towards embracing expansion.

Developing authentic relationships with one's self and with others encourages us to be whole within ourselves. Authenticity promotes self-respect, honesty and integrity. For any relationship to be successful, there must be mutual trust and respect. Without trust, we would be too afraid to share aspects of ourselves that might make us vulnerable. By not sharing aspects of ourselves for fear that what has been revealed might be used against us in conflicts, we make ourselves emotionally unavailable, and inevitably, curtail intimacy. The trust and honesty that we build in our relationships should make us feel sufficiently secure to share our lives, thoughts, feelings, frustrations and deepest secrets with our partners without worrying that those secrets will be betrayed. We should be able to bare our souls without the fear of being attacked, criticized, demeaned or denigrated. We need to be comfortable enough in our relationships to be true to ourselves, without compromising our values, truth and self-worth.

As Jason and I believe in the inherent goodness of people and therefore in each other, we are able to forgive the other easily knowing that any hurt caused is, more often than not, unintentional. Neither one of us has crossed personal boundaries with the other as both of us respect not only each other's personhood but also each other's need for personal space and time. I appreciate the love and companionship that Jason and I share. He has brought humour and laughter into my life. He is the yin to my yang, and when I am with him, I feel a need to slow down. Jason has laughingly pointed out several times that he sees me as the 'hare' and himself as the 'tortoise.' We try to meet in the middle ground, with me slowing down, and him speeding up. Given some of our personality and lifestyle differences, Jason and I continue to work towards a compromise, which allows us to respect each other's space and lifestyle.

I have come to realize that when we allow love to flow into a negative situation or conflict, there is often no need for power struggles, envy, competition and personal attacks. Instead, there is a joining of heart, soul, spirit and mind. I am trying, in my spiritual walk, to incorporate this realization into my daily life through my mindfulness meditation practice.

I have also begun to perceive relationships as holy encounters. As much as they offer us valuable lessons and experiences that we can grow from, they also provide us with the opportunity to be the love that we are. No matter what happens in our lives or how painful our challenges, we can choose to radiate love, peace and healing to ourselves, to others and to any situation we may find ourselves in. The choice we make to grasp life is always a choice towards conscious expansion.

The adversities I have experienced in my life have awakened me to my spiritual path and to my true Self. They have empowered me emotionally and spiritually. My sense of discernment has been developed and refined; I have greater understanding of the self and clarity concerning my life's purpose. We often go through a dark season when we experience tragedies, humiliation, failures, rejections and hurts but it never remains dark if we consciously choose to recreate ourselves by allowing the light of grace to dispel the darkness and gloom.

Growth is a choice. Growth is love that impels us to keep moving forward to fulfil our heart's desires; it is the love that ignites the passion in every fibre of our being. The more we align ourselves with love, compassion and forgiveness and surrender to the flow of grace, the more empowered we become in exercising choices that are right for us.

Chapter 21

He who experiences the unity of life sees his own self in all beings, and all beings in his own self, and looks on everything with an impartial eye.

Buddha

Unity Consciousness: Love Thy Neighbour as Thyself

The underlying precept of forgiveness and change is consciousness. To be conscious is to be aware of how our thoughts, beliefs and choices influence the way our life unfolds. In addition to being conscious of how we define and understand our relationship to ourselves, to our Creator, to others, to the earth and to all living forms, we also need to be aware of how we discharge our civic and social obligations.

Consciousness is through the Sacred Heart. It is in the heart that we attune ourselves to the higher powers of unity: respect, kindness, integrity, honesty and charity. Abiding by these principles not only makes a positive difference in our own lives, but also in the lives of others. Since our thoughts emit powerful energetic frequencies that impact the collective consciousness of humanity, we have a responsibility to live a conscious life.

Living a conscious life therefore entails living a life based on the principles of unity consciousness, which encompasses experiencing all life force as interconnected. Unity consciousness celebrates the essence of oneness, of one spirit. It upholds the belief that since we are all members of 'one body' or parts of a whole, regardless of our religious faith or beliefs, we are interconnected. It is this realization of interconnectedness that induces us to move beyond conflict, disharmony, resistance and polarities. Boundaries and barriers that manifest as differences, divisions and separations will disintegrate. There is no longer the perception of 'we versus them' but of 'us.' There is inclusivity rather than exclusivity.

Since the unity that we feel with others as fellow human beings motivates us to view them as we would view ourselves, it creates awareness in us that other people face problems just like we do and these are no less important than our own. This inevitably evokes in us respect and compassion for others as we learn to recognize that each and every one deserves our love and forgiveness and not condemnation and judgment. Judgment objectifies the other and separates the other from us, thereby impeding the divine flow in us.

Compassion, on the other hand, helps us to view our perpetrators not as our enemies and our situations as a war between 'us and them.' Instead, compassion allows us to see beyond the transgression to their humanity, to their human foibles and imperfections. In understanding the dynamics of a dysfunctional relationship, which often mirrors the warring elements within the individuals involved, we come to see that our perpetrators, like us, have acted in unconscious and unkind ways from inner pain, fear and insecurity. People who are in pain and are critical of themselves tend to project this criticism onto others. Unable to accept themselves, they do not accept others. Similarly, we ought to be aware that there may be facets of ourselves that we do not accept and that we have subconsciously invited people who reflect our own lack, non-acceptance and discontent into our lives.

All forms of abuse and social evil, whether in the private, public or global arenas, can therefore be perceived as a desperate call for love and grace. Perceived differences in any form is a failure to respect the oneness of spirit and the interconnectedness of humanity. When we participate in a culture of unforgiveness, revenge, retaliation, hatred, prejudice, bias, persecution or any form of atrocity, we break the bonds of unity consciousness and align ourselves with the essence of separation and division. It is our mind and not our heart that reinforces this separation, which in turn creates spiritual disconnection that keeps us mired in pain.

Thus by attuning to our heart, we can align ourselves to the oneness of spirit and see the humanity in our perpetrators. It is grace that prompts us to correct errors and resolve tensions, problems and conflicts, not through violence and revenge, but with love, compassion and forgiveness. Ultimately, it is love alone that leads to right action. By upholding the principle of unity, that I and the other are the same in essence no matter what our external differences, we will perceive our 'neighbours,' who may be our brother, partner, a perpetrator or a stranger, as no different from us. As William Blake writes in his poem "The Divine Image":

> *And all must love the human form,*
> *In heathen, Turk, or Jew;*
> *Where Mercy, Love, and Pity dwell*
> *There God is dwelling too.*

Aligning ourselves with unity consciousness therefore empowers us to transcend differences and to extend forgiveness to our perpetrators. In choosing to forgive, we exercise the choice to differentiate the act from the person. Life is sacred! It is imperative that we end our stories of our victimization. In Emmanuel Kant's words, "It is not only God's will that we should be happy, but that we should create our own happiness." It is mostly gratitude and reverence for the sacredness of life that paves the way for happiness to manifest in our lives. Gratitude is the choice of one who is attuned to their true Self.

I am constantly reminded to surrender my battle with the flow of life and to be in the present moment, to revel in my being as I claim my space in this world to be the love that I am. I feel the passion, the confidence and excitement for life as I take every opportunity to grow and experience life to the fullest.

I have come a long way in my life's journey, empowered by the challenges I have had to face in life. I no longer feel sequestered or overwhelmed by my past experiences and have emerged from the flaming forest, eager to fulfill my soul's purpose. Life has a way of directing us forward by placing synchronistic connections and experiences before us, which can open new doors for us if we heed the summons from within.

As I have broadened my perspective of life, a result of having transcended the limits in how I had defined my reality, I have come to separate Steven's past behaviour from his identity, recognizing the fact that he has changed over the years as I have. I have forgiven both him and myself for the all-consuming drama that we had played out in our relationship. Although we walked through the flaming forest in our marriage, we have emerged from it on amicable terms. When we leave a relationship with love and forgiveness rather than with hate and revenge, we nourish our soul and that of the other. Steven and the children too have a better relationship now, with more communication. They appreciate that he continues to provide financial support for their university education. As for my siblings, even though they are aware of what had transpired between us, they focus, as I do, on the goodness in him.

Most of us will at one point or another walk through the flaming forest in our life's journey through our trials and tribulations. This may take myriad forms: divorce, illness, accident, loss of a loved one, broken relationships, loss of job, loss of property and addictions. These crises often provide us with the opportunity to die to our old self and to be reborn to our new self; they provide us with the chance to empower ourselves, to grow and to expand, and to get in touch with our true Self. Our soul will keep prodding us to awaken us to our potentiality, to our creativity, to our abundant self, to fulfil our true purpose in life.

Until we heed the clarion call of the universe, it will rain down boulders on us to make us return to the source of our being. Paying attention to the inner voice of our soul will return us to our Sacred Heart, to balance and harmony. It will help us to fine-tune our discerning abilities to make the right decisions and to execute the right action, thereby restoring congruence within ourselves.

The healing that has taken place in me helps me to reach out to others. I have learned to break down boundaries of fixed notions of how life should be, how people should behave, and what defines success in our materialistic and success-oriented world. I am learning to let go of judgment of myself and of others. When healing is done through committed inner work on oneself and through conscious interaction, it propels us into a higher space of love.

The law of forgiveness returns us to serendipity as we go through the process of releasing our past enslavements and distorted perceptions. In doing so, we move into an abiding state of grace, ignited by our unity consciousness. There is power in compassion, power in forgiveness, power in gratitude. But the greatest power of all is the power of authentic love.

I have walked through the refining fire of the flaming forest and have emerged from it as a stronger and compassionate person, with a capacity to love deeply and with a new found zest for life. There is, without doubt, life beyond the flaming forest, for what can sprout from the ashes of the refining fire but new growth, vitality, rebirth!

Epilogue

My Spiritual Journey: I Am Who I Am

Stacy and the three other women's courage to come forth to 'speak the unspeakable' and to assume responsibility for their own healing and growth is an endeavour in embracing the sacredness of life. Each of them has, in their own way, ventured into that deep mysterious inner territory, which has given birth to their creative expression and enabled them to embark on a journey of transcending their reality of abuse and betrayal.

There have been times in my life when I have ignored divine guidance, much to my detriment, but in writing this book, in celebrating the women's stories, I have come forward to honour my soul's direction to help others in a similar plight to regain their power, to let them know that no situation is insurmountable.

My encounter with the metaphysical world, or with what cutting-edge sciences now refer to as the cosmic memory field, began when I was a little girl with the manifestation of mystical incidents that I have now come to understand as 'akashic experiences.' Leading systems theorist Ervin Laszlo, author of the **Akashic Experience**, defines this as "a lived experience in the extra- or non-sensory mode." It is a mode in which the experiencing subject transcends the physical body of the five senses to consciously or subconsciously access information from the cosmic memory field. These subliminal experiences can occur in various forms: as intuition, synchronistic occurrences, premonition, near-death experiences, out-of-body experiences, visions, or as spontaneous or miraculous healings.

Some of my early akashic experiences include not only being able to sense if something bad was going to happen to me or to my family members, but also being aware of the presence of discarnate spirits. As I began to intensely pursue an inner spiritual life, my akashic experiences expanded to include the phenomenal. These experiences have awakened me to my soul's calling. As I look back on my life, I realize how synchronistic patterns of occurrences have prepared me for this journey.

In September 2003, caught in a cycle of despair and desperation over the many personal challenges I was facing, I prayed fervently to God to show me the way forward. I was stuck and needed help in moving forward with my life. As I immersed myself deeply in meditation, a vision of Jesus Christ in a hooded cape appeared before me. I looked into his warm, brown eyes and felt His love and compassion. Although awe-struck, I was filled with an abiding sense of calmness and assurance.

It was also during this period that I had two brief 'out-of-body' experiences during meditation. In those phenomenal moments, I was imbued with ineffable bliss, embraced completely by pure light. I felt ecstatic. From a higher vantage point, I was conscious of looking down at my lifeless body and saying to myself: "That's my body. I'm dead." Although conscious of the fact that I was peering down at what was merely the shell of my body, I felt very much alive, vibrant and conscious of my thoughts and surroundings. I remember feeling a deep reluctance to return to my physical body but found myself, all too soon, back in it. The experiences made me aware of myself as pure consciousness and made me realize that death is illusory. These mystical experiences left me with an intense desire for a deeper connection with God.

In the midst of more akashic experiences, I kept receiving the message to write this book and was told that I would be guided in the direction and structure the book was to take. So I began writing sporadically from 2007 and completed my first draft in late 2010 while working, caring for my severely ill daughter, going through a couple of healing crises myself and doing my essential inner work. As I journeyed through this phase, things about my life and my soul purpose became clearer to me. I am eager for this book to reach out to the many others who are broken in spirit, for it to show them the way towards a cathartic journey into self-awareness, healing and transformation.

Personal transformation is absolutely integral to elevating social and global consciousness. Only when the shadow of the individual is embraced by its light, can its light go forth to awaken the soul of the world. And as more individuals turn inward to transform and awaken, to understand and speak the language of the soul, the whole planet will begin to sing with the grace of light.

Bibliography

Abrahams, Hilary. *Supporting Women after Domestic Violence: Loss, Trauma and Recovery.* Kingsley, Philadelphia, London. 2007.

Advocates for Human rights. "Prevalence of Domestic Violence." *Stop Violence against Women.* A Project of the Advocates for Human Rights, n.d. Web. 15 May 2012. <http://www.stopvaw.org/domestic_violence2.html>.

Beattie, Melody. *Codependent No More.* Hazelden, Minnesota, USA. 1987.

Blake, William. "The Divine Image." *Norton Anthology of English Literature.* Volume 2. 8th Edition. Ed. Stephen Greenblatt. Norton, New York, USA. 2006.

Bloom, Michael V. *Adolescent-Parental Separation.* Gardner, New York, USA. 1980.

Bowlby, John. *Attachment and Loss.* Volume 1. Basic, New York, USA. 1969.—. *Attachment and Loss.* Volume II. Basic, New York, USA. 1973.

Braden, Gregg. *The Spontaneous Healing of Belief.* Hay House, California, USA. 2008.

Briggs, Dorothy Corkille. *Celebrate Yourself: Enhancing Your Own Self-Esteem.* Doubleday, New York, USA. 1977

Burney, Robert. *Co-dependence: The Dance of Wounded Souls.* Joy to You & Me, California, USA. 1995.

Cixous, Hélène. "The Laugh of the Medusa." *Literature in the Modern World: Critical Essays and Documents*. Ed. Dennis Walder. Oxford, London, UK. Singapore. 1990.

A Course in Miracles. Original Edition. Ed. Helen Schuman and William T. Thetford. Course in Miracles Society, Nebraska, USA.

Dalai Lama, and Howard C. Cutler. *The Art of Happiness*. Coronet, London, UK. 1998.

Emoto, Masaru. *The Hidden Messages in Water*. Trans. David A. Thayne. Beyond Words, Hillsborough, Oregon, USA. 2005.

Evans, Patricia. *The Verbally Abusive Relationship*. Adams Media Corporation, Avon, Massachusetts, USA. 1992.

—. *Verbal Abuse Survivors Speak Out*. Adams Media, Avon, Massachusetts, USA. 1993.

Farrel, Bill, and Pam Farrel. *Love, Honour and Forgive*. InterVarsity Publishers, Downers Grove, Illinois, USA. 2000.

Green, Glenda. *Love Without End: Jesus Speaks*. Spiritis, Sedona, USA. 1999.

Hay, Louise L. *You Can Heal Your Life*. Hay House, California, USA. 1984.

Hazan, Cindy, and Philip R Shaver. "Broken Attachments: Relationship Loss from the Perspective of Attachment Theory." *Close Relationship Loss: Theoretical Approaches*. Ed. Terri L Orbuch. Springer-Verlag, New York, USA. 1992.

Holy Bible. English Standard Version. Good News, USA. 2001.

Hubbard, Barbara Marx. *Conscious Evolution: Awakening the Power of Our Social Potential*. New World. California, USA. 1998.

Jacobi, Jolan. *The Psychology of Jung*. Trans. B.W.Bash. Foreword. C.G.Jung. New Heavens, Yale University, USA. 1943.

Jung, C. G. *Psyche and Symbol: A Selection of Writings of C. G. Jung.* Ed. Violet S. de Laszlo. Anchor-Doubleday, New York, USA. 1958.

Kapoor, Sushma. *Domestic Violence against Women and Girls. Innocenti Digest* 6 (June 2000). UNICEF Innocenti Research Centre, Florence, Italy. Web. 15 May 2012. <http://www.unicef-irc.org/publications/pdf/digest6e.pdf>.

Laing, R.D. *The Divided Self: An Existential Study in Sanity and Madness.* 1959. Penquin, London, UK. 1990.

Laszlo, Ervin. *The Akashic Experience: Science and the Cosmic Memory Field.* Inner Traditions, Vermont, USA. 2009.

Luskin, Fred. *Forgive for Good.* Harper Collins, San Francisco, USA. 2002.

McTaggart, Lynne. *The Field: The Quest for the Secret Force of the Universe.* Harper Collins, New York, USA. 2002.

Murphy, Joseph. *The Power of Your Subconscious Mind.* Revised by Ian McMahan. Bantam, New York, USA. 2000.

Myss, Caroline. *Sacred Contracts: Awakening Your Divine Potential.* Three Rivers, New York, USA. 2002.

Norwood, Robin. *Women Who Love Too Much.* 1985. Pocket, New York, USA. 1990.

"Dictionary." *Oxford Dictionaries.* Web. 15 May 2012. <http://oxforddictionaries.com/>.

Porter-Efron, Ronald and Patricia S Potter-Efron. *The Emotional Affair: How to Recognise Emotional Infidelity and What to Do About It.* New Harbinger Oakland, Canada. 2008.

"Protecting Against Abuse, Exploitation and Violence." *A World Fit for Children Statistical Review* 6 (2007). *Progress for Children* series. UNICEF. Web. 15 May 2012. <http://www.unicef.org/

progressforchildren/2007n6/files/
Progress_for_Children_-_No._6.pdf>.

Spring, Janis Abrahms and Michael Springs. *After the Affair.* Harper Collins, New York, USA. 2006.

Stone, Joshua David, Phd. *Soul Psychology: Keys to Ascension.* Light Technology, Flagstaff, USA. 1994.

Tolle, Eckhart. *A New Earth.* Penguin, London, UK. 2005.

"Violence Against Women." *Intimate Partner and Sexual Violence Against Women.* World Health Organization (WHO). Web. September 2011.<http://www.who.int/mediacentre/factsheets/fs239/en/

Women Against Violence Against Women (WAVAW). Newsletter. November 2011.

Weiss, Elaine. Ed.D. *Surviving Domestic Violence: Voices of Women Who Broke Free.* Volcano, California, USA. 2004.

Wiley, Eleanor with Caroline Pincus. *There are No Mistakes.* Conari-Red Wheel/Weiser, York Beach, ME, USA. 2006.

Williams, Nick. *Powerful Beyond Measure.* Bantam, London, UK. 2003.

Williamson, Marianne. *The Gift of Change.* Harper Collins, New York, USA. 2004.

—. *Everyday Grace.* Bantam, London. 2003.

About the Author

Sasha Samy has a background in education. She holds an M.A in English, diplomas in education and TESL, and certificates in counselling psychology, psychotherapy, and energy healing modalities. She has taught at an American college and one of the universities in Singapore. Samy has published poems in a national newspaper, literary magazines and in newsletters as well as in an anthology. Her volunteer work has included working at a woman's organization, fundraising for a hospital outreach group and facilitating an English practice group for immigrants to Vancouver. Born in Singapore, Sasha Samy now resides in Vancouver with her two children and husband.

Visit Sasha Samy at www.sashasamy.com

CPSIA information can be obtained at www.ICGtesting.com
Printed in the USA
LVOW13s1926300913

354768LV00001B/170/P

9 781770 673847